Getting
People
on Board

The Results-Driven Manager Series

The Results-Driven Manager series collects timely articles from *Harvard Management Update* and *Harvard Management Communication Letter* to help senior to middle managers sharpen their skills, increase their effectiveness, and gain a competitive edge. Presented in a concise, accessible format to save managers valuable time, these books offer authoritative insights and techniques for improving job performance and achieving immediate results.

Other books in the series:

Teams That Click

Presentations That Persuade and Motivate

Face-to-Face Communications for Clarity and Impact

Winning Negotiations That Preserve Relationships

Managing Yourself for the Career You Want

Taking Control of Your Time

Dealing With Difficult People

A Timesaving Guide

THE RESULTS-DRIVEN MANAGER

Getting
People
on Board

Harvard Business School Press

Boston, Massachusetts

Copyright 2005 Harvard Business School Publishing Corporation

All rights reserved

Printed in the United States of America
09 08 07 06 05   5 4 3 2 1

Library of Congress Cataloging-in-Publication Data

The results-driven manager: getting people on board.
    p.   cm. — (The results-driven manager series)
    ISBN 1-59139-636-0 (alk. paper)
    1. Leadership. 2. Organizational change. 3. Employee motivation.
I. Title: Getting people on board. II. Harvard Business School Press
III. Series.
HD57.7.R47 2005
658.4′092—dc22

                                                    2004011829

The paper used in this publication meets the requirements of the American National Standard for Permanence of Paper for Publications and Documents in Libraries and Archives Z39.48-1992.

Contents

Contents

Contents

Getting
People
on Board

Introduction

. . .

More and more of today's managers at all levels in their organizations are talking about needing to "get people on board." But what does getting people on board mean, exactly? At its core, it means motivating employees to support the changes their company must make in order to remain competitive in a rapidly shifting business world and to solve its most pressing problems. How do you know when all of your team members are "on board"? There are several signs:

- People feel energized and alive.

- They have a sense of purpose.

- Team members know where they're going and why it's important to get there.

- Your direct reports understand your company's strategy and how their own efforts fit into it.

Successfully getting all of your people on board adds up to crucial results for your firm. Moreover, getting people on board is more important today than ever before. Why? Problems come faster and are more complicated than in previous decades, and change is now constant. Indeed, most large companies have dozens of initiatives under way simultaneously. Mergers and acquisitions, along with new technologies, products, and markets, have all further increased the already ever-present pressure on managers to whip up enthusiasm, energy, and creative thinking among their subordinates.

A Daunting Challenge

But getting people on board isn't easy. Change often comes as an ongoing stream of challenges that simultaneously represents both danger and opportunity. As a manager, you have to know how to avoid the dangers while also seizing the opportunities. You also need to identify which organizational traditions to conserve and which to let go.

Getting people on board is challenging for other reasons as well. For one thing, you're asking people to change the things they hold dear: their daily habits, ways of working, relationships, and approaches to analyzing and solving problems. Many people find this kind of change painful, even excruciating. As a result, your group may connive to oppose change—in ways that can leave you at a loss or unable to lead.

Resistance to change may come in numerous forms, making it even harder for you to overcome it and maintain your position as a leader. For instance, people may marginalize you—as one group did when it encouraged a female executive to lobby for work/life issues rather than drive other "hardcore" changes that were more important to the firm at the time. Or, they might try to take you out of action by using several tactics—such as diverting your attention with a trivial issue, attacking your character, or dangling a different initiative in front of you that they know you'll find especially appealing.

The Essence of Leadership

Clearly, to avoid these perils and get your people on board, you need to move carefully and thoughtfully. Your ultimate aim is actually twofold and forms the core of leadership: communicate a compelling vision and purpose for action, while you help your group solve the company's most pressing problems. Those problems may involve anything from sustaining stock prices and streamlining costs, to keeping the troops motivated during tough economic times or some other strategic challenge.

Even the most revered and respected leaders find that fulfilling these responsibilities can prove difficult at times. But as the articles in this collection reveal, help is at hand—from management experts, researchers, and practicing managers who deal with these challenges every day. If you want to get *your* people on board—and keep them there—you can learn to master the following skills:

- Blending a variety of leadership styles so as to leverage each style's strengths and use the right style for the right situation

- Combating resistance to change from your team or department

- Communicating clearly, continually, and compellingly about your company's most serious problems and the changes needed to solve them

The three sections in this volume focus on these crucial skills and offer you a wealth of practical guidelines for how to sharpen them. Here's a preview of what you'll find as you explore the articles.

Mastering the Right Blend of Leadership Styles

Business writer Nick Morgan starts the book's first section with "Are You Getting the Best Solutions for Your Problems?" Citing the work of management expert Christopher Hoenig, Morgan describes six leadership styles, each with its own strengths and weaknesses. The best leaders, Morgan writes, mix and match these approaches to leverage the styles' strengths and compensate for their weaknesses.

This article will help you decide whether you tend to be an *innovator* (you see potential where others see only pain), a *discoverer* (you're familiar with new terrain), a *communicator* (you build, nurture, and draw sustenance from human relationships), a *playmaker* (you make things happen and guide your team to resolution of problems), a *creator* (you construct solutions that hold together under pressure), or a *performer* (you deliver practical results). Morgan also explains how to blend these styles for the best outcome—for instance, by reminding yourself to attend to community building while driving for results, or by remembering that process and product are just as important as the positive team dynamics you're cultivating.

In "Teresa M. Amabile on How Leaders Influence Creativity," the Harvard Business School professor further explores the idea of mixing leadership styles. In Amabile's view, "effective leaders integrate task and relationship management." To manage tasks, leaders "focus on getting the job done: clarifying roles and responsibilities, planning and organizing projects, and monitoring the work." To manage relationships, leaders "focus on the socio-emotional: showing consideration of subordinates' feelings, acting friendly and personably to them, and being concerned for their welfare." When leaders mix these two aspects of management, their teams feel supported—a key element in getting people on board.

Business writer Jennifer McFarland shines the spotlight on a particularly potent leadership style in "Leading Quietly." Describing the work of Debra Meyerson,

Associate Professor of Education at Stanford University, McFarland maintains that sometimes the best way to get people on board is to make "small, slow, incremental changes" rather than big, dramatic moves. Meyerson terms leaders who use this approach "tempered radicals." This style, she adds, is especially effective for managers who "represent ideals or agendas that are somehow at odds with the dominant culture" of their company.

In some change efforts, getting people on board requires gaining cooperation from others over whom you have no formal authority. For example, perhaps you're heading up a cross-functional implementation team whose members don't report directly to you. Or maybe you're managing a set of outside vendors who will play a critical role in a new information technology initiative. The article "How to Lead When You're Not the Boss" introduces the "lateral leadership" style that's so essential to this kind of situation.

As the article suggests, real leaders' effectiveness stems not from formal authority but from "a handful of attributes, attitudes, and habits that set [them] apart from others." These qualities include "who you are"—that is, you have a reputation for hard work and integrity; "what you know"—you've acquired significant new facts or insights; and "how you interact with people"—you solicit others' input, offer your ideas as part of a solution, and model or demonstrate the changes you're advocating. Armed with these qualities, you lead laterally by establishing clear goals, carefully analyzing situations, learning from experience, engaging people in tasks that need doing, and providing feedback in the form of simple appreciation or questions that help others identify ways to improve their performance.

In the final article in this section, business writer Lauren Keller Johnson interviews London Business School professor Jay Conger to gain additional insights into the lateral leadership style. "Lateral leadership," Conger maintains, "counts among any manager's most essential skills." Conger describes the "constellation of capabilities" managers need to practice lateral leadership—including *networking* (cultivating relationships with the people inside and outside your company whose support you need to carry out change initiatives), *persuasion and negotiation* (creating agreements with people that offer mutual benefits), *consultation* (visiting people whose buy-in you need, and asking their opinions about the initiative you're championing), and *coalition building* (gaining support from people who will be most affected by your change initiative).

Overcoming Resistance to Change

Managers not only get people on board by knowing how to blend leadership styles for the best effect, but by overcoming resistance to change. This section opens with the article "Surviving Leadership." In this selection, management professors Ronald A. Heifetz and Marty

Linsky argue that before managers can effectively lead change, they must first avoid the dangers that come with resistance. The process starts with "getting on the balcony"—stepping back amid the action of a change initiative and asking, "What's really going on here?" and "How do people seem to be feeling?" Understanding the varying perspectives among any factions you've identified, and finding partners who can support you against resisters, can lay the groundwork for surmounting resistance. And remember: Study your opponents even more carefully than you evaluate your supporters.

Business writer David Stauffer describes additional tactics for overcoming resistance in "How to Win the Buy-In." Whether resistance takes the form of natural ambivalence toward major change or active opposition, you can get people on board with these strategies:

1. TELL IT LIKE IT IS. Disclose the reason for change openly, honestly, and completely, providing the "brutal facts" indicating why change is crucial.

2. BREAK THE INITIATIVE DOWN INTO MANAGEABLE CHUNKS. Separate a multiyear change project into discrete phases or steps, each with its own interim goals. Smaller, bite-sized projects help you win commitment by showing momentum and progress.

3. HEAR EMPLOYEES OUT. Listen to people's concerns, to determine whether resistance is taking the form of "I don't get it," "I don't like it," or "I don't like you," and then identify ways to address these emotions.

4. REVERSE THE FLOW. Invite creative ideas and input from all levels in the organization, to cultivate a sense of ownership of the initiative among employees.

The next two articles in this section explore the power of small, early successes to help overcome resistance to change. In "Fostering Change While Avoiding the Road to Martyrdom," editor Loren Gary stresses the importance of using small wins as catalysts for larger transformations. To illustrate how this works, Gary describes how a young manager at a financial firm carried out his commitment to hiring minorities by quietly asking valued new minority managers to make a similar commitment in their own hiring practices—and to actively maintain mentoring relationships with those hires. The process that this manager launched with tiny steps resulted in the hiring of 3,500 minority employees. And now that the manager is in the executive ranks, he can address issues of diversity much more actively and openly.

Clearly, small successes can yield big results. But how precisely can you score those early, deceptively modest wins? Harvard Business School professor Michael Watkins addresses this question in "New Leadership Role?" Watkins offers three practices for securing early successes:

1. ESTABLISH A-ITEM PRIORITIES—the major objectives your change initiative must achieve. Then brainstorm ideas for potential early wins that will most move your group toward those longer-term goals.

2. IDENTIFY A "CENTER OF GRAVITY"—one key area or process where early wins are probable and will yield the most substantial performance improvement.

3. INITIATE PILOT PROJECTS—specific initiatives within the center of gravity that score early successes.

Another key to overcoming resistance is enabling your people to lead change by themselves—and thus feel a greater sense of ownership over an initiative. With ownership comes a greater ability to embrace change. In "Companies Don't Develop Leaders, CEOs Do," University of Michigan professor Noel Tichy offers guidelines for developing leaders at every level in your organization. Though Tichy is speaking specifically about CEOs in the interview from which this article is drawn, he maintains that managers at all levels can cultivate leadership in others. He describes several ways to do so, including gathering wisdom about "products, services, distribution channels, market dynamics, and all the other components of running a business," and then cultivating that knowledge in less-experienced minds.

Loren Gary echoes this same theme in the final article in this section, "Neoteny: How Leaders Recruit the Right Kind of Followers." Citing numerous experts, Gary poses the question, "How can leaders recruit independent-minded initiative-takers to the cause?" The process starts with becoming a "first-class noticer"—that is, recognizing hidden significance and opportunities in business changes, as well as spotting talent in people. When you're "alive to what is new in the current situation and to how contexts may have changed," you cause others to see that you're attuned to the present and are therefore trustworthy. "Followers see that their willingness to take initiative [amid] uncertainty will be welcomed. And in exercising that initiative, they are developing their [own] leadership skills."

Communicating Effectively About Change

Knowing how to blend leadership styles and being able to overcome resistance to change aren't sufficient skills on their own to get people on board for a major change effort. You also have to communicate effectively about change. The articles in the third and final section of the book provide techniques and strategies for conveying a compelling message about why change is valuable to your company and how your people can turn an alluring vision of a better future into current, concrete reality.

Communications consultant John Baldoni starts things off with "Effective Leadership Communications." In many experts' view, Baldoni maintains, "communication is the backbone of leadership. Without constant communication, you have no leadership." Baldoni recommends eight steps to initiate effective leadership communications, including delivering a consistent message; setting clear, credible goals; issuing calls to action; and choosing the right communication channels (e-mail, meetings, face-to-face conversations, etc.).

In "Making an Impact," David Stauffer focuses on how to use your appearance, stature, and bearing to augment the power of your message about change. Something as simple as smiling can exert an enormous impact on how others respond to you. An athletic stance—shoulders down and back, and feet about shoulder-width apart—can communicate confidence and authority. And clearly defining your goals can gain you a visible—and infectious—measure of enthusiasm.

In addition to stature and bearing, "framing"—that is, focusing your people's attention on specific aspects of a change effort—can be a potent technique for communicating about change. As MIT faculty member Melissa Raffoni explains in "Framing for Leadership," framing enables you to influence how employees view and respond to the change effort you're advocating. Framing "brings clarity to complexity" and helps employees navigate around obstacles to change. It can also help you refocus a team discussion on the crucial aspects of a change initiative. For example, suppose that the discussion wanders off track during a meeting about an initiative involving price changes. In this case, you might reframe simply by saying something like, "Let's keep in mind that the question is whether we need to lower our prices."

To decide how to frame your message about change, Raffoni recommends asking yourself a specific set of questions before every communication. Such questions include "What is the purpose of my communication?"; "What do I want my listeners to think, feel, or do after hearing my words?"; "How will my message affect my team?"; and "How can I communicate in ways that increase my credibility?"

The subject of the emotional component of communicating about change receives additional attention in the article "How to Get People on Board." For example, one expert recommends connecting the change with objectives that employees care most about. These "hot buttons" vary across individuals: "Techies," for instance, may "get excited about the feeling that they're out on the bleeding edge doing cool stuff. Salespeople and other competitors like the idea of winning in the market-place." Other team members may care most about delivering great service to customers. "Depending on the context, you may be able to get people fired up about any of these objectives—or about others, such as the chance to earn a fat bonus or learn new skills." The key? Help people feel that "there's something more here than simply earning more money for shareholders."

Connecting emotionally and communicating effectively about change requires what researcher Daniel Goleman has called emotional intelligence (EI). In the section's final article, "Becoming a Resonant Leader," Loren Gary draws from Goleman's, and other experts', work on this topic. Leaders with high degrees of EI, the experts agree, have "the ability to articulate a group's shared yet unexpressed feelings and to give voice to a mission that inspires others."

Emotional intelligence comprises four basic competencies: 1) *self-awareness* (you have the ability to read your own emotions and accurately assess your personality's impact on others), 2) *self-management* (you keep disruptive emotions under control, and you're trustworthy, flexible, and optimistic), 3) *social awareness* (you know how to empathize with others' concerns), and 4) *relationship management* (you inspire, persuade, and resolve disagreements).

According to researchers, managers can improve their EI through self-directed learning: "intentionally developing or strengthening an aspect of who you are or who you want to be, or both." How? First, define your ideal self—who you want to be. Then, figure out what you're actually like and where your strengths and weaknesses lie. Next, devise a learning agenda for leveraging your strengths while addressing weaknesses. Then, experiment with and practice new behaviors, thoughts, and feelings "to the point of mastery." Finally, develop supportive and trusting relationships that enable you to sustain these changes.

There's no doubt about it: Getting people on board for a major change in your organization takes a broad array of skills and healthy doses of determination and focus. But as the articles in this collection make clear, you have numerous techniques, tools, and tactics at your disposal for enhancing and exercising your change-leadership abilities. Learning to put these resources into action is well worth your time and energy.

When you've finished reading the selections in this volume, ask yourself how you might begin applying what you've learned in your company. For example:

- What leadership style do you generally use? How well has that style served you, your team, and your firm in the past? How might you incorporate additional styles into your repertoire, so that you can better motivate your people—and those people who are not your direct reports— to support change?

- What kinds of resistance, if any, have you encountered from people when you've advocated change efforts in the past? What might you do differently during a future change initiative that might boost your chances of overcoming resistance?

- How do you usually communicate about change to your employees? What seems to work well about the communication techniques you use? What doesn't work well? With future change initiatives, what might you do differently to communicate more powerfully?

By honing your leadership talents, knowing how to recognize and overcome resistance to change, and communicating effectively about change, you'll go a long way toward not only getting people on board—but also keeping them there. Your reward? A team of enthusiastic, creative, initiative-taking supporters who can help your company survive *and* thrive in a fast-changing, competitive world.

Mastering the Right Blend of Leadership Styles

• • •

Managers who succeed in getting people on board epitomize the core responsibilities of leadership. In other words, they communicate a compelling vision and a purpose for carrying out the changes that will enable their company to solve its most urgent problems. They also learn and master a blend of leadership styles and adapt these styles depending on the circumstances at hand.

In this section, you'll read about a palette of leadership styles and discover how to mix them in highly effective ways. By blending styles, you will be able to build community and personal commitment among your direct reports while creating hard-core, measurable results for your company.

As you read about the different leadership styles in the articles in this section, ask yourself which styles best describe you. Are you an "innovator," a "communicator," a "tempered radical," or a "lateral leader"? Determine your natural tendencies—then use the strategies in these selections to integrate several additional styles into your repertoire. The payoff for mastering a blend of styles? A flexible, versatile approach that enables you to get *your* people on board.

Are You Getting the Best Solutions for Your Problems?

• • •

Nick Morgan

You get paid to solve problems. And these days problems come thicker and faster than ever: sustaining the stock price, deciding about layoffs, keeping the troops motivated, managing capital risk, trying to focus on a brighter future. How do you radiate sufficient confidence and authority without sounding smug or unaware? How do you paint the picture of an optimistic future without glossing over the very real pain of the present?

Most managers embody one of six leadership styles, says Christopher Hoenig, author of *The Problem Solving Journey: Your Guide to Making Decisions and Getting Results.* It's a wise manager that knows how she comes across to her employees. Indeed, the essence of leadership is communicating a vision and a purpose for action. The rest is, in fact, problem solving.

Morgan D. Jones, author of *The Thinker's Toolkit: 14 Powerful Techniques for Problem Solving,* argues that the essence of successful problem solving is to be willing to consider real alternatives. If you're too locked into a way of thinking or a communication style, you may not be able to open up enough to consider alternatives, and your problem-solving skills will suffer accordingly. Jones, who is also a former CIA analyst, says, "To solve problems . . . we must learn how to identify and break out of restrictive mindsets and give full, serious consideration to alternative solutions. We must learn how to deal with the compulsions of the human mind that, by defeating objective analysis, close the mind to alternatives. Failure to consider alternatives fully is the most common cause of flawed or incomplete analysis."

Hoenig identifies six types of problem solvers; the secret to good problem solving, then, is to know the weaknesses of your own style and to fight against them by cultivating alternate ideas and viewpoints.

The Innovator Versus the Discoverer

As Hoenig says, "Innovators view the world in a special way. They see potential where others see only pain. They envision the mountain top, even when they're in the valley." The challenge for the Innovator is to make real and practical those tempting visions.

Similarly, the work of a Discoverer is found in that uncertain new terrain. Hoenig says, "Knowing a territory—the work of a Discoverer—means acquiring the right knowledge about the critical elements of the environment you solve problems in. Discoverers ask the best possible questions and get timely information about their terrain." But they also need to keep in mind that not everyone shares their passion for the quest. Most people would rather stay in familiar territory than risk breaking new ground.

Former Visa International president Dee Hock is perhaps the quintessential Innovator. Where others saw an ever-mounting tide of bad debts in the credit card industry of the late 1960s, Hock saw an opportunity for collective action. Hock communicated a simple vision of a new order: a universal currency managed collectively. But this painfully shy man communicated largely by listening to others and enlisting them in his vision by incorporating their ideas into his own.

21

The result, after an enormous amount of struggle, was Visa, which has grown by 10,000% and now covers the globe and has 500 million clients.

If you're an Innovator, you need to incorporate other visions into your own—much as Hock did. Work these visions together into a story that communicates where you're headed, and you'll be on the way to achieving the kind of communicative power that Hock showed.

If you're a Discoverer, you'll need to balance your passion for knowledge with a concomitant concern for the well-being of your troops. In large part, that's a matter of knowing their strengths and weaknesses as well as your own.

Also, don't let your enthusiasm carry you away into forgetting the importance of having a thoroughgoing plan. Curb your impatience and make sure you hear from more than one expert about the road ahead.

The Communicator Creates Trusting Relationships

Hoenig says, "Communicators know how to build, nurture, and draw sustenance from the essential fabric of human relationships. Some relationships are transitory—making quick exchanges with strangers or crossing paths infrequently with acquaintances. But long-term problem solving requires building deep, rich relationships." This relationship building is what Communicators excel at. They can forget that all the relationship building in the world won't actually build a house—or a company. You also need a plan.

The challenge, if you're a Communicator, is not to forget that process and product are as important as the team. In forming your solutions, bring in the talents of process- and product-oriented people so the goals are not forgotten.

The Playmaker Makes Things Happen

Hoenig says, "A problem solver needs to get oriented to the choices, prioritize and select what to work on, plan and initiate action on the most urgent opportunities, and guide a team through the stages of resolution. This is the realm of the Playmaker."

Secretary of State Colin Powell's success with America's Promise, a not-for-profit organization launched with the U.S. Chamber of Commerce to mentor young people in summer jobs, shows the skills of a Playmaker. Powell inspires, cajoles, prods, and arm twists his way through corporate America on behalf of today's youth.

Playmakers tend to value people for what they do, not for who they are. Playmakers are constantly trying to make the strategy work. They may become so busy using people that they may not notice that people need attention, too. Playmakers in the middle of a communications crisis over a falling stock price and messy layoffs, for example, should take time along the way to celebrate small victories with the troops that remain—or risk losing their loyalty.

The Creator Designs Optimal Solutions

Says Hoenig, "The bigger and tougher and more competitive your problem is, the more challenging it is to design, build, and evolve solutions that will hold together under pressure and over time. This job is the province of the Creator."

> Failure to consider alternatives is the most common cause of flawed or incomplete analysis.

John Sawhill was a university president, a partner in a global consulting firm, and a senior cabinet official before he became the head of The Nature Conservancy. On his watch, the nonprofit organization realized that buying land to save it from development was not working, because the larger ecosystems were still suffering.

And so, under Sawhill, The Nature Conservancy began to focus on the "Last Great Places," working with many organizations to manage whole ecosystems.

That's how a Creator approaches her work: taking stock of what assets and resources she possesses, and figuring out how best to deploy them. It's a complicated and challenging task, one that requires the ability to not get lost in the day-to-day issues that threaten to kill forward momentum. If you're a Creator, your communication challenge is to help your employees stay focused on that larger picture, even though you may love getting your hands dirty in the design of the details. Your understanding of the vision is implicit, but you need to make it explicit in order to keep others motivated. You also need to understand that designing a solution is not the same thing as achieving it; for that you need the skills of a Performer.

The Performer Delivers Practical Results

"Performers are the hard-bitten, practical characters who are always willing to get their hands dirty to make things happen," says Hoenig.

Isabelle Autissier is a Frenchwoman who has triumphed in the Vendée Globe, a solo nonstop sailing race around the world. As Hoenig says, "One of the more extraordinary aspects of the execution skills of sailors like Autissier is their ability to find simple, effective resolutions to the problems they face along the way. . . . They are experts at dreaming up repair schemes that are viable enough to allow them to complete the race."

The Performer is the leader who can react on the fly, figuring out how to keep the team functioning or rejuvenate the IT system that seems hopeless to everyone else. And it's in that ability to keep things moving that the communication strengths and weaknesses of the Performer are to be found.

The urgency of the task is always in front of the Performer, and he can sometimes forget the community around him. Moreover, while it is second nature to the Performer to understand how to keep driving toward the end result, he will at times forget that others need to be reminded of the big picture. Performers need to remind themselves to take time to repair the team with words of encouragement and healing when a particularly rough patch has been got through.

So Which Are You?

An Innovator who can see a future most cannot—and needs to remember to focus on the here and now? A Discoverer whose curiosity about the road ahead can lead you to push your troops hard—sometimes too hard? A Communicator whose ability to foster human connections needs to be leavened with a practical sense of focus on the task at hand? A Playmaker who sees how to put it all together, and sometimes needs to slow down and tend to the needs of his team? A Creator whose ability to find new solutions amidst the challenges of the moment sometimes overpowers her future vision? Or a Performer, who gets the job done, sometimes to his own personal cost and to those around him?

Jones says, "We settle for partial solutions because our minds simply can't digest or cope with all of the intricacies of complex problems. We thus tend to oversimplify, hopping from one problem to another like jittery butterflies, alighting briefly and only on those elements we can comprehend and articulate." Sometimes the only way to fight this tendency is to force yourself to speak through your weaknesses, not your strengths.

For Further Reading

The Problem Solving Journey: Your Guide to Making Decisions and Getting Results by Christopher Hoenig (2000, Perseus)

The Thinker's Toolkit: 14 Powerful Techniques for Problem Solving by Morgan D. Jones (1998, Three Rivers Press)

Reprint C0201D

Teresa M. Amabile on How Leaders Influence Creativity

* * *

We often assume that leadership, especially charismatic leadership, plays a central role in spurring creativity and innovation. But there's little empirical basis for this belief, says Teresa M. Amabile, Edsel Bryant Ford Professor of Business Administration at Harvard Business School. She and her colleagues Elizabeth Schatzel, Giovanni Moneta, and Steven Kramer studied the daily diaries of members of 26 high-powered project teams headed by middle managers. The researchers were struck by the profound ways in which a manager's ordinary, routine interactions with subordinates can support—or undermine—creativity.

How crucial is it for leaders to generate creative ideas or suggestions?

Most of the successful leaders we studied did not, by their own behaviors, directly inspire creative ideas in the people they were leading—they didn't present some lightning-bolt idea that then sparked team members' creativity. Instead, there was an intervening process whereby seemingly trivial behaviors that leaders engage in on a day-to-day basis would have a profound indirect influence.

We found that much of what these leaders said and did led team members to feel either more or less supported by the leader. That perceived leader support seemed to influence creative work down the road. We theorize that high levels of leader support are important for creativity because they influence people's sense of ownership and competence in the work, which leads to deeper, more motivated involvement in the work.

So is a focus on task management what really matters?

Task-oriented behaviors focus on getting the job done: clarifying roles and responsibilities, planning and organizing projects, and monitoring the work. Relationship-oriented behaviors focus on the socio-emotional: showing consideration of subordinates' feelings, acting friendly and personably to them, and being concerned for their welfare.

But every leader behavior, no matter how task-oriented, is likely to convey information about the leader-subordinate relationship. Similarly, even the most relationship-oriented behavior is likely to have consequences for the subordinate's task engagement. Effective leaders integrate task and relationship management.

In this regard, I don't think the management literature has paid sufficient attention to the ways in which leadership can fail. Our analysis of team members' diary entries revealed that the negative leader behaviors evoked more emotionality than the positive behaviors. Moreover, the absence of a negative behavior often caught the subordinate's attention, whereas the unexpected absence of a positive behavior tended to go unnoticed.

OK, let's look at the negative behaviors first.

The negative form of three behaviors—monitoring, problem solving, and clarifying roles and responsibilities—were the key correlates of diminished feelings of leader support: micromanaging the details of high-level subordinates' work, failing to address difficult technical or interpersonal problems, and giving assignments without sufficient regard for the capability or other responsibilities of the subordinate receiving them. Stopping these negative behaviors could yield significant improvements in subordinates' thoughts, feelings, and creative performance.

And which behaviors did the most to promote feelings of leader support?

There were four: monitoring effectively (obtaining information about the progress of a project without undercutting the subordinate's sense of autonomy), consulting (demonstrating an openness to subordinates' ideas), supporting (helping alleviate stressful situations, keeping members informed), and recognizing (showing empathy for subordinates' feelings, especially their need for recognition).

Monitoring shows up as both a key negative and a key positive behavior.

That's right. Subordinates, contrary to popular opinion, don't just want leaders to get out of their way; instead, they want a particular kind of monitoring. The contrast here is not between micromanagement and doing nothing, it's between micromanagement and consultation. Consultation is very important to subordinates: They want to be given responsibility, but they also want the leader to keep in touch, to ask for their views, to ask about issues that she can help with.

Reprint U0312D

Leading Quietly

•   •   •

Jennifer McFarland

A mid-level executive at a large American automotive corporation was concerned about the impression his company was making in the countries where its manufacturing plants were located. He was also convinced that the company could build facilities more efficiently by using local talent and resources. Charged with building a new plant in Mexico, he hired local architects to design a building that would reflect the tastes of the local community. The new facility—and by extension, the company as a whole—earned the locals' respect. As the ties to the community strengthened, the company's ability to hire and retain local workers grew noticeably—all because someone who marched to a slightly different drummer seized an opportunity to improve the organization.

This story highlights the importance of an often over-looked type of leader: the *tempered radical*. Debra Meyerson, associate professor of education at Stanford University, defines tempered radicals as "organizational insiders who contribute and succeed in their jobs. At the same time, they are treated as outsiders because they represent ideals or agendas that are somehow at odds with the dominant culture." Capitalizing on this tension between insider and outsider status, tempered radicals effect "small, slow, incremental changes" that can add up to something very significant.

The best-led companies, says Noel M. Tichy, professor of organizational behavior and human resource management at the University of Michigan's Graduate School of Business, are the ones that develop leaders throughout the organization. And potential leaders are embedded in every level, he insists—if only an organization's leaders can spot them. Although the press lionizes charismatic, heroic examples of leadership, a quieter, less egotistical approach—one characterized by the ability to teach and learn from a wide variety of people and the willingness to support the subtle transformations wrought by tempered radicals—is actually better suited to the everyday challenges of running a business.

The Willingness to Get Punched in the Nose

In today's knowledge economy, "the game is about brains and aligning the brains in your company," declares Tichy. As a leader, "your number-one task is being a leader-teacher." Unfortunately, most companies are "outsourcing leadership education to the worst people: professors and consultants." But the real damage here lies in the lost opportunity. A genuine leader-teacher "absorbs as much information from the learner as the learner does from the teacher," Tichy explains. So if you're not teaching others, you're missing out on the chance to learn from them.

"Most CEOs that I know go to their middle management programs and broadcast. They don't come and learn," Tichy states. But General Electric's former chairman Jack Welch provides a shining counterexample. GE's annual reports recount the story of how the company revised its mandate to be either number one or number two in any market—or get out of the business: "It took a mid-level company management training class reporting out to us in the spring of 1995 to point out—without shyness or sugar-coating—that our cherished management idea had been taken to nonsensical levels. They told us we were missing opportunities and limiting our growth horizon by shrinking our definition of the market." At the three-year planning review that July, GE's leaders were asked to change the definition of their markets, says Tichy. Now, unit heads would be able to look beyond being number one or number two in a market and to enter businesses where GE's market share was 10% or less.

Who was responsible for what the annual report calls "this punch in the nose"? Middle managers, replies Tichy—they opened Welch's eyes to the possibilities. Welch's willingness to abandon the famous "one-or-two" mantra that had served the company so well was a major factor in the double-digit revenue growth rates GE achieved in the late 1990s. Tichy draws several lessons from this example:

- Welch had a mindset that placed great importance on teaching.

- Welch had "a teachable point of view"—he was willing to change his mind, even about something to which he had been very committed.

- Welch imparted to his managers the courage to stand up to him, to take him on.

This combination of teaching and leading with a teachable point of view "altered the course of the whole company," says Tichy. "It helped GE become smarter and better aligned."

Everyday Performance Art

"Leadership is to a great extent a performing art," says Warren G. Bennis, a distinguished professor of business administration at the University of Southern California's Marshall School. It involves "the capacity to engage people" (see box, "Learning from Gloria Swanson"). "When Franklin Roosevelt was introduced to Orson Welles, FDR said, 'Mr. Welles, you are the greatest actor in America.'

Learning from Gloria Swanson

"The definition of leadership is to have inspired, ener-gized followers," says Warren G. Bennis, distinguished professor of business administration at the University of Southern California's Marshall School. And nothing inspires followers like knowing that you're listening to what they say. The reverse is also true, as the following examples of failed leadership demonstrate.

Douglas Ivester, who succeeded the beloved Roberto Goizueta as CEO of Coca-Cola, didn't make himself visible when a product-tampering scare erupted in Belgium. When his company was trying to buy the French company Orangina, Ivester didn't think it was important to talk face-to-face with Orangina's execu-tives—Coca-Cola lost out in this widely publicized acquisition attempt. And perhaps most damning, he ignored entreaties to hire a person with strong people skills (to complement Ivester's financial orientation)

And Welles replied, 'No, Mr. President, *you* are.'" But by no means do you need an international reputation to exercise leadership. Everyday leaders—Debra Meyerson calls them tempered radicals in her book of the same name—often fail to show up on the radar screen because they occupy the lower echelons of the organization chart or work "in very quiet ways."

as his number-two executive. Ivester lasted only 18 months at the helm.

At Compaq, Eckhard Pfeiffer helped bring about his own demise by refusing to listen to ideas that contradicted his own.

The eponymous military leader in Shakespeare's play *Coriolanus* was loath to mingle with the public. He saw it as pandering and "felt he would be sacrificing his integrity and authenticity if he said things that didn't come naturally to his lips," says Bennis. "He was killed by his own people."

In the movie *Sunset Boulevard*, Gloria Swanson's character laments, "I am big. It's the pictures that got small." Like Swanson's character, Ivester, Pfeiffer, and Coriolanus lacked an adaptive capacity, says Bennis: "They could not abandon their own egos to the talents of others. They listened only as long as the world was in line with what they were saying." And they were emotionally tone-deaf, not only with respect to themselves but also with respect to the way the world was changing.

Tempered radicals take a variety of forms. Some advance an agenda of social responsibility—fair trade, for example, or environmentalism, gender equity, or diversity. "But there are also people who advance product innovations, who want to make the workplace more creative in an organization that feels oppressive," says Meyerson. "They exist throughout the organization, and they struggle with how much they can rock the boat and at the same time stay inside of it and get ahead." Their leadership consists of "the kind of pushing-back they do on a system. That is, they stand for something that is fundamentally different. They speak a different truth than that which is dominant in the organization. They question assumptions and conventions. Despite lots of setbacks and struggles, they have in them a conviction to something bigger than their own success, and they persist in whatever way they can."

Working with Tempered Radicals

Because they're not completely in tune with the organization's culture, tempered radicals "can be really important sources of learning" for the organization, Meyerson adds—which is why it's important for you to be attuned to who they are and what they're thinking.

Make It a Priority to Ask Around

"If your job is finding new ideas, helping to nurture them, and leading the organization to adapt, then you shouldn't view the search for everyday leaders as an add-on responsibility," declares Meyerson. "It's an essential part of what you have to do." Go beyond your immediate circle, to "places where you've never been in the organization and ask around: Who has made a difference? Who thinks differently? Who comes from a different background?"

Reward Truth-Telling

"You don't necessarily shine a flashlight on" tempered radicals, cautions Meyerson. "You don't necessarily want to make them heroes of the next great truth—particularly if you're not prepared to protect them and what they stand for." But you can send signals that it's okay for them to say what they believe. Meyerson tells the story of a managing partner of a New York law firm who flew a promising second-year associate across the country to listen to her advice about how the firm should be managed. The story spread throughout the firm, and as a result, this event "really marked the woman's career," Meyerson observes. "It gave her the confidence to speak the truth."

Henry Mintzberg, professor of management studies at McGill University in Montreal, believes that Americans are obsessed with the leadership style personified by John Wayne in Western films. "The extent to which Americans need heroes," he says, "is absolutely mind-blowing." He has a point—but our need for heroes probably won't go away anytime soon. Those who want to emulate the less dramatic style of leadership discussed here, however, can take heart. John Wayne also made a movie about a championship boxer who renounced the ring and returned to his ancestral home in Ireland. It was called *The Quiet Man.*

For Further Reading

"E-Leadership, Take Two" by Melissa Raffoni (*Harvard Management Update*, June 2001)

"Six Keys to Training Your Successor" (*Harvard Management Update*, February 2001)

Reprint U0107B

How to Lead When You're Not the Boss

*　　*　　*

Where is that chain of command when you need it? If you're like most managers, you regularly find yourself in situations where you have responsibility but not authority to get things done through a group. Maybe you head up a cross-functional team whose members don't report to you. Maybe you manage a set of outside vendors. Or maybe you do have nominal authority, but find that your charges—software engineers, hotshot Gen X marketers, whoever—respond to directives the way a cat responds to the command "roll over."

In all such cases, issuing direct orders is part of the problem, not part of the solution. As Peter Drucker puts

41

it, "you have to learn to manage in situations where you don't have command authority, where you are neither controlled nor controlling."

So what works? As it happens, a few students of leadership have sketched out approaches designed for precisely this situation. Harvard negotiation specialist Roger Fisher and colleague Alan Sharp dub their model *lateral leadership* or "leading from the side." Jay A. Conger, professor of organizational behavior at the London Business School and formerly the executive director of the Leadership Institute at the University of Southern California's business school, advocates *management by persuasion,* noting that the most effective managers he observed during research and consulting assignments "actually shied away from issuing directives." Whatever the specifics, these are approaches that can be learned and practiced by anyone, boss or not.

The Must-Haves of Leadership

Real leadership, of course, has never been a matter of mere formal authority. Leaders are effective when other people acknowledge them as such—by listening seriously to their ideas, valuing and following their suggestions for action, and turning to them for advice. What makes a leader isn't a title, it's a handful of attributes, attitudes, and habits that set him or her apart from others.

Who You Are

Everyone's familiar with the "born" or charismatic leader. But what most aspiring leaders need isn't charisma, it's more mundane virtues such as a reputation for hard work and integrity. In your colleagues' perception, asks Conger, have you always done what you said you'd do? Do they think of you as "someone who always tells the truth and admits his mistakes?" These traits alone won't make you a leader, but a lack of them will surely eliminate you from contention.

What You Know

You've seen it happen: A meeting is meandering, the outcome uncertain—and then one participant introduces significant new facts or insights. Bingo: Information carries the day. Occasionally the information provider is smarter or more experienced than other participants. More often, she has done her homework and so knows things that others don't. It's rare that a person consistently lacking in information is acknowledged by a group as a leader.

How You Interact with People

Are you inclined to tell people what to do? Unless you really are in charge you're unlikely to elicit their cooperation—

indeed, colleagues may resist your instructions precisely because they don't like being told what to do by someone who isn't their boss. Instead of telling, Fisher and Sharp suggest asking questions to solicit others' input, offering your ideas as part of a solution, and doing something that models or demonstrates what you'd like to see happen. If you're advocating a cost-cutting initiative, for example, spend some time researching one particular line item and propose some ways to reduce it.

Applying Leadership Skills

There's obviously much more to leadership—even lateral leadership—than these three habits of behavior. Fisher and Sharp lay out a useful five-step method for learning to be a lateral leader; it can be applied to virtually any project, team, or meeting in which you're a participant.

1: Establishing Goals

People accomplish the most when they have a clear set of objectives. It follows that any group's first order of business is to write down exactly what it hopes to achieve. The person who asks the question, "Can we start by clarifying our goals here?"—and who then assumes the lead in discussing and drafting those goals—is automatically taking a leadership role, whatever his or her position.

2: Thinking Systematically

Observe your next meeting: People typically plunge right into the topic at hand and start arguing over what to do. Effective leaders, by contrast, learn to think systematically—that is, gathering and laying out the necessary data, analyzing the causes of the situation, and proposing actions based on this analysis. In a group, leaders help keep participants focused by asking appropriate questions. Do we have the information we need to analyze this situation? Can we focus on figuring out the causes of the problem we're trying to solve?

3: Learning from Experience— While It's Happening

Teams often plow ahead on a project, then conduct a review at the end to figure out what they learned. It's more effective to learn as you go along, which means that part of a group's daily work is to conduct mini-reviews of its work to date and make any necessary mid-course corrections. Why is this ongoing process more effective than an after-action review? The data are fresh in everyone's mind. The reviews will engage people's attention because the group can utilize its conclusions to make adjustments. Here, too, anyone who focuses the group on regular review and learning is playing a de facto leadership role.

4: Engaging Others

A high-performing group engages the efforts of every member, and effective group leaders seek out the best fit possible between members' interests and the tasks that need doing. Suggest writing down a list of chores and matching them up with individuals or subgroups. If no one wants a particular task, brainstorm ways to make that task more interesting or challenging. Help draw out the group's quieter members so that everyone feels a part of the overall project.

5: Providing Feedback

If you're not the boss, what kind of feedback can you provide? One thing that's always valued is simple appreciation—"I thought you did a great job in there." Sometimes, too, you'll be in a position to help people improve their performance through coaching. Effective coaches ask a lot of questions ("How did you feel you did on this part of the project?"). They recognize that people may try hard and fail anyway ("What made it hard to accomplish your part of the task?"). They offer a few suggestions for improvement, being careful to explain the observation and reasoning that lie behind them.

The days are long past when managers could expect to climb the ladder to leadership merely by sticking around and not making waves. Today, you need to start leading wherever you happen to be. Both you and your company will benefit.

For Further Reading

Getting It Done: How to Lead When You're Not in Charge by Roger Fisher and Alan Sharp (1998, HarperBusiness)

Winning 'Em Over: A New Model for Management in the Age of Persuasion by Jay A. Conger (1998, Simon & Schuster)

Reprint U0003A

Jay Conger on Exerting Influence Without Authority

• • •

Lauren Keller Johnson

Congratulations—you've been asked to lead a change initiative! But there's a catch—its success hinges on the cooperation of several people across your organization over whom you have no formal authority.

If you're like most managers, you're facing this sort of challenge more often these days because of flatter management structures, outsourcing, and virtual teams. For those reasons, a greater number of managers now need to get things done through peers inside and outside their organizations. In this age of heightened business complexity, moreover, change itself has grown increasingly complicated. A majority of change initiatives now involve multiple functions within and even between companies, and many such efforts encompass an entire firm.

New kinds of partnerships and alliances have emerged as well, and they require managers to exercise influence over peers from the other companies. Santa Clara, California-based Applied Materials, for example, has 800 engineers and other employees working inside Intel, collaborating daily with their Intel partners to develop successful new products.

In such circumstances, command-and-control leadership—the "I leader, you follower" approach—doesn't get a manager very far. Jay A. Conger, professor of organizational behavior at the London Business School and formerly the executive director of the University of Southern California's Leadership Institute, points out that managers and executives at all levels must use a more lateral style of leadership.

Why Lateral Leadership?

Lateral leadership, Conger maintains, counts among a manager's most essential skills, and comprises a constellation of capabilities—from networking and coalition building to persuading and negotiating.

Though honing these skills takes time and patience, the payoff is worth it. That initiative you're championing will stand a far better chance of being implemented quickly. You'll gain access to the resources you need to carry out the effort. You'll see doors swing open freely to the key players whose cooperation you need most. And perhaps most important, you'll achieve the central purpose of managerial work: getting things done through other people—and catalyzing valuable change for your organization.

A Constellation of Capabilities

So how do you begin mastering the skills that constitute lateral leadership? Conger recommends focusing on four closely interconnected and mutually reinforcing capabilities.

Networking

Cultivate a broad network of relationships with the people inside and outside your company whose support you need to carry out your initiatives. If networking doesn't come naturally to you, create a personal discipline through which to acquire this capability. Conger maintains that "certain people are portals to other people—they can connect you to more and bigger networks. You need to build relationships with these individuals in particular."

Constructive Persuasion and Negotiation

Too many managers, Conger says, wrongly view persuasion and negotiation as tools for manipulation. But conducted with an eye toward mutual benefit, they can vastly enhance your influence.

To make persuasion and negotiation constructive rather than manipulative, view the person you're dealing with as a peer instead of a "target." Take courses and read books on these subjects to hone your skills. And find a seasoned colleague within the company who can serve as a confidant and brainstorming partner.

Consultation

Take time to visit the people whose buy-in you need. Ask their opinions about the initiative you're championing. Get their ideas as well as their reactions to your ideas.

Too many managers, Conger says, rush to define a series of steps that they believe constitutes the right way to carry out their initiative. They then circulate around the company and try to impose their solution on others—mistakenly believing that they're engaging in productive consultation.

The result? Resistance and bickering over process details. "You'll get far better results," Conger says, "if you commit to and advocate the desired outcome but invite peers to participate in defining the process for achieving that outcome."

Coalition Building

It's a fact of human nature that several people who are collectively advocating an idea exert more influence than a lone proponent. For this reason, coalition building plays a vital role in lateral leadership. By building coalitions, Conger explains, you gather influential people together to form "a single body of authority."

To assemble a powerful coalition, begin by asking yourself who's most likely to be affected by the change you're proposing. Whose "blessing" do you need—whether in the form of political support or access to important resources or individuals? Whose buy-in is crucial to your initiative's success?

The Challenges of Lateral Leadership

Though lateral leadership consists of several concrete, interrelated skills, many managers cannot easily master those capabilities. For one thing, Conger points out, they're often so focused on their own functional silo that they don't know who beyond their own internal group should be included in their networking and coalition-building efforts.

To combat this "functional focus," take time to find out who makes things happen in your organization. Whom do people go to for advice and support? And who tends to throw up roadblocks to new ideas and changes? You won't find the answers to these questions in the organizational chart. As Conger says, you gain a sense of these things through informal contact and casual get-togethers with colleagues throughout the company.

> **Find out who makes things happen in your organization.**

In addition to focusing too closely on their own function, managers experience intense pressure to grapple with what they see as responsibilities more urgent than building relationships. After all, many of them are rewarded for producing concrete, short-term results, Conger notes, whereas investments in lateral-leadership "capital" can take time and patience—and often the dividends don't come until much later.

So how do you reconcile the need to produce in the short run with the equally important need to lay the groundwork for productive collaboration in the long run? Conger recommends dedicating a specific amount of time each day or week to sharpening your lateral-leadership skills. For example, commit to having lunch each Thursday with a different person inside or outside your organization whom you don't know well but who may play an important role in a project you'll be leading.

Conger also recommends getting to know influential people before starting to work with them on a project. For instance, suppose you'll be leading a project that will involve managers from several other functions and you've scheduled a formal kick-off meeting in a month. Seek out those managers in the weeks leading up to the meeting and ask them for their thoughts about the upcoming project.

Creating the Right Environment

Considering the increasing need for lateral leadership—and its unmistakable benefits—you might assume that companies are moving energetically to train managers in this important area. But, Conger notes, that isn't the case.

To be sure, many firms offer courses on influence, circulate articles on various aspects of lateral leadership, and establish mentoring programs designed to help managers identify and access "portals" quickly. But formal training and mentoring efforts can have mixed results, Conger warns.

Why? "Successful lateral leadership grows out of positive chemistry between people. You can't predict or control the natural affinity people have for one another—that glue that makes relationships of mutual influence possible."

Rather than "matching people up" through a formal mentoring program, companies have far more success by creating opportunities for people to mingle—and then letting them forge mentoring and networking relationships on their own. Conferences, seminars, and company-sponsored social events provide opportunities for people to get to know peers with whom they might not otherwise interact.

Chemistry becomes even more important, Conger adds, in virtual teams. In these increasingly common work groups, members have few chances to meet face to face and engage in the "sizing up" that humans do instinctively. Without these nonverbal exchanges, people can't build the trust that makes lateral leadership possible. Thus, people on virtual teams must be particularly intentional about their networking. Face-to-face meetings—even if they require expensive travel—are often well worth the cost. Lunches, coffees, and other casual social gatherings can further cement working relationships.

As the business landscape continues to shift, companies will need managers who can exercise lateral leadership with increasing skill and confidence. But because many firms still don't invest explicitly in cultivating this talent throughout their workforces, managers would do well to take the initiative themselves.

Reprint U0312E

Overcoming Resistance to Change

• • •

In your career as a manager, you've likely encountered one or more forms of resistance from employees while trying to get them on board for a major change effort. Change is painful and difficult and people have developed numerous tactics for avoiding it. Perhaps your team has paid lip service to the initiative, but then never followed through on the actions needed to move the effort forward. Or, equally frustrating, maybe they've tried to derail you by diverting your attention with trivial issues or even going so far as to attack your character.

The articles in this section will provide you with a wealth of tools, techniques, and practices you can use to overcome resistance to change—no matter what shape that resistance takes. These antidotes range from breaking initiatives down into manageable chunks and building momentum through small, early successes—to cultivating a sense of ownership of the change effort among your subordinates while enabling them to become change leaders in their own right.

Similar to the effects that come with expanding your repertoire of leadership styles, when you master a potent mix of strategies for combating resistance, you boost your chances of inspiring personal commitment to change from even your most recalcitrant employees.

Surviving
Leadership

* * *

"When you lead people through difficult change, you challenge what people hold dear—their daily habits, tools, loyalties, and ways of thinking—with nothing more to offer perhaps than a possibility," write Ronald A. Heifetz and Marty Linsky. Their book, *Leadership on the Line: Staying Alive Through the Dangers of Leading* (Harvard Business School Press, 2002), provides a sobering analysis of how organizations connive to oppose change—and how leaders get bruised, or even destroyed, in the process. Heifetz, founding director of the Center for Public Leadership at Harvard's Kennedy School of Government, and Linsky, faculty chair of many of the school's executive programs, spoke with *Harvard Management Update* editor Loren Gary about how leaders can overcome organizational resistance.

How does resistance to adaptive change—the kind of change that requires people's hearts and minds to change—manifest itself?

Heifetz: When exercising leadership, you encounter four forms of resistance: marginalization, diversion, attack, and seduction. When people resist adaptive work, their first goal is to shut down leadership in order to preserve what they have. An adaptive challenge requires an organization to separate what's precious—what should be held onto—from what is expendable. Of course, at the start of adaptive work, many people feel that everything is precious; they're reluctant to give up anything.

Each of the four forms of resistance has its subtleties. For example, marginalization can occur when women in male-dominated institutions are encouraged to carry the gender issue for the whole organization—that is, to do all the lobbying for pay equity, or work/life issues, or the full inclusion of women in senior management. Marginalization can also happen to those at the top: Sometimes leaders collude unwittingly with their marginalizers by delaying the pain of a necessary transition.

Linsky: With diversion, there are many ways in which communities and organizations will consciously or unconsciously try to make you lose focus. They sometimes do this by broadening your agenda, sometimes by overwhelming it, but always with a seemingly logical reason for disrupting your game plan. When you're attacked, the goal of the attackers is to submerge the issue you are advancing by turning the subject of the conversation to your character or style, or even to the attack itself. Seduction, the fourth form, connotes any process by which you get taken out of action by an initiative likely to succeed because it has a special appeal to you.

Your underlying point about all four of these forms is not to take them personally, but to understand the function they serve.

Heifetz: Yes, these forms of resistance reduce the disequilibrium that would be generated were people to address the adaptive issues. They seek to take the adaptive issues off the table, to maintain the familiar, restore order, and protect people from the pains of adaptive work.

Linsky: Leaders are rarely neutralized for personal reasons. The role you play or the issue you carry generates the reaction. For the most part, people criticize you when they don't like the message. Still, it's difficult to resist responding to the personal attack. But exercising leadership often means bearing such scars. Moreover, being aware of the likelihood of receiving opposition is critical to managing it when it arrives.

So what are some of the strategies and tactics for mobilizing adaptive work?

Heifetz: It starts with getting on the balcony. This image captures the mental activity of stepping back in the midst of action and asking, "What's really going on here?" Few tasks strain our abilities more than putting this idea into practice. Without some perspective on the bigger picture, you are likely to misperceive the situation and make the wrong diagnosis, leading you to misguided decisions about whether and how to intervene.

Linsky: We all get swept up in the action, particularly when it becomes intense or personal. Picking up the overarching patterns is very tough when you're also taking part in the action—the most difficult part to notice is what you do yourself. When you're on the balcony, try not to jump to familiar conclusions. See who says what. Watch the body language. Watch the relationships and see how people's attention to one another varies: supporting, thwarting, or listening.

And after you've climbed up to the balcony?

Heifetz: You have to return to the dance floor if you want to affect what's happening. Staying on the balcony in a safe observer role is as ineffective as never achieving that perspective in the first place. The process must be iterative, not static. Next, you need to understand where people are—you can't lead them forward if you don't know that. Both your survival and your success depend on your skill at reaching a true understanding of the varying perspectives among the factions. Their view is likely to be different from yours, and if you don't take their perspective as the starting point, you are liable to be dismissed as irrelevant, insensitive, or presumptuous.

Linsky: You also need to listen to the song beneath the words. People naturally, even unconsciously, defend their habits and ways of thinking and attempt to avoid difficult value choices. Thus, after hearing their stories, you need to take the provocative step of making an interpretation that gets below the surface.

Heifetz: Read the behavior of the organization's authority figures for clues. Look at them as you would through a window, understanding that what you are seeing is really behind the plate of glass. The trap is thinking that the senior authority figure is operating independently and expressing a personal point of view. In fact, that person is trying to manage all the various factions, and what you observe is a response to the pressures he or she is experiencing.

What do you mean when you write that "the merits of a cause and the strategy used to move it forward are relevant but not controlling"?

Linsky: Successful leaders in any field emphasize personal relationships. Leaders have to think politically—in particular, they need to find partners. Admittedly, there can be internal pressures, inside of you, that resist joining forces. Partners might push their own ideas, compromising your own; connecting with them takes time, slowing you down. And working with a group might dilute your leadership—that can be a drawback if it is important that you get the credit for an initiative, or if you want to reassure yourself and others of your competence.

Heifetz: Still, you need partners. They provide protection; they create alliances for you with factions other than your own. And partners who are members of the faction for whom the change is most difficult can be especially significant. But partnerships are not unlimited, unconditional, or universal. A natural ally agrees with you on your issue and is willing to fight for it, but that doesn't mean she'll abandon all other commitments. If you forget about how these commitments influence your partner, you run the risk of undermining your effectiveness and destroying the alliance.

What about those who oppose you?

Linsky: People who oppose what you are trying to accomplish are usually those with the most to lose by your success. Changing sides will cost them dearly in terms of disloyalty to their own roots and constituency. But it may cost nothing for your allies to come along. For that reason, your opponents deserve more of your attention, as a matter of compassion as well as a tactic of strategy and survival.

Most of us cringe at spending time with and taking abuse from people who do not share our vision or passion. Too often we take the easy road, ignoring our opponents and concentrating on building an affirmative coalition. But keeping your opposition close connects you with your diagnostic job. If it is crucial to know where people are at, then the people most critical to understand are those likely to be most upset by your agenda.

Got any advice about holding your coalition together?

Heifetz: The people who determine your success are often those in the middle; they resist your initiative merely because it will disrupt their lives and make their futures uncertain. When leading such people, the first thing to do is realize that if you've been in a senior role for a while and there's a problem, it is almost certain that you are part of the reason it has not yet been addressed.

You need to identify and accept responsibility for your contributions to the current situation, even as you try to move your people to a different, better place. You also need to acknowledge the losses that will come with the adaptive changes you're seeking. When you ask people to do adaptive work, you may be asking them to confront internal contradictions between their espoused values and their actual behavior. This essentially requires people to be disloyal to their roots. Whenever you ask people to do that, there's going to be anguish. Leadership requires reverence for these pains of change and recognition of the manifestations of danger, but it also calls for the skill to respond.

Linsky: Sometimes, verbal acknowledgement of the losses you're asking people to accept is not enough—you have to model the behavior you're asking them to learn. The modeling is often more than symbolic: It can involve taking real risks. But even symbolic modeling behavior can have substantial impact.

So the behavior modeling becomes a way of showing people that all the losses and sacrifices will be worthwhile?

Heifetz: Right, you've got to show them the future. People are willing to make sacrifices if they see the reason why. Communicate, in every way possible, why people need to sustain losses and reconstruct their loyalties. People need to know that the stakes are worth it.

Linsky: At the same time, you have to be willing to accept casualties. When organizations and communities go through significant change, some people simply cannot or will not go along. But if you signal that you are unwilling to take casualties, you present an invitation to the people who are uncommitted to push your perspective aside.

Reprint U0203C

How to Win
the Buy-In

* * *

David Stauffer

A middle manager's initial reaction to organizational change is often to suspend judgment, says Mike DeNoma, CEO of the global consumer banking unit of Standard Chartered Bank. "Then, when there's so much as a hint of any trouble, they'll gladly jump in to attack your effort and devastate it."

Standard Chartered Bank, popularly known as Stan-Chart, is a venerable international bank that has long focused on emerging markets, particularly in Asia. It has about $100 billion in assets, approximately 30,000 employees, and some 750 offices in more than 55 countries. DeNoma has been leading StanChart's $80 million international CRM installation project since 2001. This effort has gone well because it's been carefully constructed and implemented with meticulous attention to the factors that help a change initiative gain buy-in from middle management.

The most helpful tool in this effort has been a so-called usability laboratory, where every proposed change of existing operations is subjected to a close-to-real-world simulation—with real frontline employees interacting with real customers. This lab has enabled managers to "see the demonstrated benefits" of changes before their full-scale implementation, says DeNoma.

There's no simple cookie-cutter method for overcoming employees' natural ambivalence toward—or even active resistance to—major change. But an investigation of three dissimilar change initiatives at three very different companies reveals that successful approaches exist.

1: Tell It Like It Is

Companies that are able to achieve breakthrough results exhibit disciplined patterns of thought, observes Jim Collins in *Good to Great* (HarperBusiness, 2001). They infuse their entire decision-making process "with the brutal facts of reality." When you start with "an honest and diligent effort to determine the truth of the situation, the right decisions often become self-evident." Similarly, the single most influential factor in a change initiative is the extent to which leaders commit from the outset to open, honest, and complete disclosure, declares John T. Malone, president and CEO of Hamot Health Foundation, which includes a 300-plus-bed hospital and nearly 2,000 employees.

In the mid-1990s, Hamot launched a change effort aimed at providing world-class medical care while maintaining financial soundness. "One of our early and essential measures was taking out a whole layer of staff from our structure—about 125 people, most of whom had been long-term, dedicated employees," Malone says. Such a large downsizing in an industry where employees have an outsized impact on customer choice and satisfaction could scuttle a nascent change effort. But frank disclosure of the downsizing and its purposes by Hamot's leaders, along with ongoing dialogue with employees and the community, averted most of the negative consequences. Since then, Hamot has won recognition in multiple categories as one of the top 100 hospitals in the United States, gained seven percentage points of regional market share, and operated consistently in the black.

Full disclosure works best by going beyond the data, analysis, and reasons: Tapping into employees' emotions is what enables a change effort to gain traction. Hundreds of interviews with people whose organizations were tackling large-scale change have led retired Harvard Business School professor John P. Kotter to conclude that "what makes these efforts work is much more a matter of an appeal to feelings than to thinking. It's showing, more so than telling, using vivid, compelling examples—in a way that delivers a smack in the gut." That effect can be achieved with appeals that follow what Kotter calls the "see-feel-change" pattern. "Compellingly *show* people what the problems are and how to resolve the problems," he and coauthor Dan S. Cohen write in their book, *The Heart of Change* (Harvard Business School Press, 2002). "Provoke responses that reduce feelings that slow and stifle needed change . . . and enhance feelings that motivate useful action. The emotional reaction then provides the energy that propels people to push along the change process."

2: Break the Initiative Down into Manageable Chunks

A multiyear change project across the organization can seem overwhelming to any one person or work group. To mitigate those effects, break the project down into discrete phases or steps, complete with interim goals. "A huge project presented to employees as smaller, bite-sized projects helps you win commitment by showing momentum and progress," says Pierre Mourier, president of Stractics Group, and an adviser associated with StanChart's CRM implementation, an $80 million program launched with a $2 million inaugural effort lim-

ited to the bank's Hong Kong market. A benefit of pro-
ceeding market by market, says StanChart's DeNoma, "is
that the next market stands on the shoulders, so to
speak, of preceding markets. We're finding this saves
time and expense as we apply ever-mounting experience
to each subsequent introduction."

"Chunking" can also lower the apparent threat level
of massive change to the managers whose buy-in is essential. The aerospace giant Lockheed Martin—the world's
No. 1 defense contractor, with annual revenues of some
$27 billion and 130,000 employees—launched "LM-21
[Lockheed Martin-21st Century] Operating Excellence" in
January 2000. Its goal was to fully integrate 18 corporate
acquisitions and to achieve lean operations, continuous
improvement, and optimum value from the customer's
perspective.

One aspect of this change effort has involved telling
managers that their control lies in bounding the problem at hand and leaving the solution to workers. "In
many managers' minds, that's equivalent to turning over
the asylum to the lunatics," says corporate vice president
and LM-21 chief Michael Joyce. "But I tell these managers that the beauty of what we're asking them to do is
that they can make small changes and then test it. 'See if
it works and, if not, you can fix it.' After I've thrown them
that lifeline, we've never yet gone back to the old ways."

All of LM-21's interim targets have now been met or
exceeded, and in October 2001 the company was named

prime contractor for the J-35 Joint Strike Fighter in the largest defense contract ever awarded.

3: Hear Employees Out

"Relationships are as important as ideas" in winning support for going in a new direction, says consultant Rick Maurer. In his book *Why Don't You Want What I Want?* (Bard Press, 2002), he classifies resistance to change in three broad categories: "I don't get it," "I don't like it," and "I don't like you." Only the first of these arises from the content of the change; it can be addressed through explanation. The other two are emotional reactions, respectively, to the change or the change messenger. Overcoming such resistance requires probing and good listening. Here, "the relationship, not the idea, is the issue," says Maurer. "Addressing the interpersonal aspects can make all the difference."

Hamot's Malone recognized that his organization's change effort would rise or fall based on top management's dedication to continual dialogue. "I went out myself and did this in front of employees and the entire community," he says. Listening well is more important than speaking well, he adds—it requires openness to everything credible. "Right now, in light of the intense national scrutiny of hospital errors, we're encouraging our staff to come forward with near misses and other concerns. We honor and reward people for doing that."

4: Reverse the Flow

"The fatal conceit" of senior management is the attempt to drive change by relying solely on top-down techniques, says StanChart's DeNoma. Lockheed's Joyce concurs: "In the West, we have all kinds of top-down management systems that are necessary and good. But to achieve excellence, we need an equally good set of tools to drive management from the bottom up."

For a change initiative at consumer electronics retailer Best Buy, a nine-member "change implementation team" became the most prominent vehicle for bottom-up influence, says Elizabeth Gibson, a change expert with consultants RHR International, who helped guide Best Buy's effort. "We had team members four levels below the top telling leaders how their behaviors were harming the change process," says Gibson. "The senior managers, to their credit, listened and responded."

The one-two punch of change driven from the top down and the bottom up creates a dynamic that consultant Mark A. Murphy calls "book-ending" the organization. Murphy, president and CEO of the Murphy Leadership Institute and adviser for Hamot's change initiative, argues that "bottom" in this context refers to customers ("your reason for being") and frontline employees ("your organization's public face"), both of which "you'd better get on board if you expect to change anything." The book-ending, Murphy says, occurs at middle management, because you've got support for the change coming down from the top and rising up from the bottom. This leads to a certain amount of discomfort, he points out, but it's discomfort of a potentially positive nature. "To the extent that leaders in the middle align themselves with the customer, employees, and CEO, middle managers can harness an almost tidal force of authority to succeed."

Even so, senior management bears the final responsibility for the change effort's success. Most change initiatives "may fail at middle management, but the reason is senior management," says consultant Robert B. Blaha, who helped design Lockheed Martin's LM-21 program. "Maybe leadership said what it wanted, but didn't provide funding to get there. Maybe they provided the required competencies and capabilities, but didn't change the metrics and rewards to evoke changed behavior. Effective senior leadership, therefore, involves finding the right levers and incentives to turn the tides of resistance into groundswells of support."

Reprint U0306A

Fostering Change While Avoiding the Road to Martyrdom

• • •

Loren Gary

"There is nothing more difficult to take in hand, more perilous to conduct, or more uncertain in its success, than to take the lead in the introduction of a new order of things," wrote the Renaissance political strategist Niccolò Machiavelli. The world is an unforgiving place, he believed, and if you want to get things accomplished, you must approach the challenges with dry-eyed realism.

But does fostering change, and surviving the effort, mean abdicating the principles you hold dear? Machiavelli's earliest critics thought him amoral in his recommendations for navigating the rough-and-tumble seas of Florentine politics. But some contemporary management assessments of his work seem to revere him for precisely the same reasons his early critics censured him. Two books, however, insist upon maintaining the link between ethics and effectiveness. Managing that link is complicated, both concede, and sometimes requires surprising tactics.

In *Tempered Radicals,* Debra E. Meyerson, an associate professor of education at Stanford University, describes people who want both "to live by their values or identities, even if they are somehow at odds with the dominant culture of their organizations," and "to succeed in their organizations." Whether the issues involve social justice—say, lobbying for the use of suppliers who pay their workers fair wages—or competitiveness—promoting a more creative and entrepreneurial culture—tempered radicals exhibit characteristics that are often absent from traditional conceptions of leadership. Their "everyday leadership," Meyerson writes, is "less visible, less coordinated, and less vested with formal authority; it is also more local, more diffuse, more opportunistic, and more humble than the activity attributed to the modern-day hero."

In *Leading Quietly*, Joseph L. Badaracco, Jr., the John Shad Professor of Business Ethics at Harvard Business

School, likens doing the right thing to a venture capital-ist's approach to investment. "Spend your political capital incrementally," he says. "Make a limited number of investments, and only after careful analysis. Manage the investment very carefully and pull out if necessary."

"Machiavelli observed that a man with no position in society cannot get a dog to bark at him," Badaracco continues. To get your cause noticed, you must have influence or standing in your company, something that isn't typically achieved by accident. This is another way in which everyday leadership differs from the altruistic, heroic model. Everyday leaders rely on a healthy dose of self-interest; it keeps them vigilant, enables them to "stay at the table" so they can continue to lead. More-over, leveraging your influence often boils down to rec-ognizing the significance of small actions. "Sometimes, in situations poised on the knife's edge," Badaracco writes, small efforts are just enough to "tip things in the right direction."

Don't Kid Yourself About the Difficulties

An old Breton prayer goes, "O Lord, the sea is so vast, and my boat is so small." The power of an organization to crush you is immense, which is why the direct approach to doing the right thing can be the road to martyrdom. Besides, says Badaracco, "there's an old saying: In life, as in war, the shortest routes are usually mined." Wisdom,

Let Us Now Praise Unsung Leaders: An Interview with Joseph L. Badaracco, Jr.

Q: In illuminating how people can minimize the dangers associated with bringing about change, do you worry that you've obscured the ethical ideal?

A: I don't know if ideals need always be so grand or need to be exemplified by people who stride across the stage of history. People need to be reminded of the importance of courage, commitment, and perseverance through real difficulties. But often the expression of the ideal is far removed from everyday life and everyday problems. What I'm trying to put in front of people could be described as a more practical or realistic set of ideals based on the efforts of people few have heard of— average people who had a sense that something was wrong, wanted to get involved, and accomplished something positive.

I think there's almost something genetic about our attraction to charismatic leaders. From earliest times, the human beings who survived were the ones who responded when some leader figure said, "The tiger's coming—here's what you need to do." We still crave those hits of inspiration; they release certain hormones that make us feel good. But the half-life of these inspiring moments is often quite short.

Instead of looking to *Fortune* cover stories for inspiration, managers need to look around them, inside their organizations. They'll see people using some version of the tactics I describe. Those people are the truly relevant role models because they're being effective in their organization—not leading a civil-rights campaign or fighting a battle at Enron. Such quiet local leaders are often the ones you can learn the most from.

Q: Is it really possible for local leaders and middle managers to speak truth to power?

A: You need to be very careful about speaking unpleasant truths to powerful people. Pronouncements of moral superiority often just get you hammered down—without making the world a better place. If you speak the truth to power in a way that undercuts your credibility or influence in an organization, you're going to be less effective on a lot of other issues. There are cases, of course, in which there's something wrong, illegal, or corrupt that has to be stopped—in those instances you have to take some real money out of the bank, put yourself at some risk, in order to put an end to the unethical behavior. But that should be your last resort, not your first one.

There are all sorts of things going on in an organization at any given point in time, and usually they are not manifestly wrong or illegal. They're just things that could be done better—for example, people maybe aren't being treated as fairly as they could be. If you want to make a difference, you've got to be a player at the table. You've got to pick your battles, find the right moment and the right words, and create the right background if you want to whisper a little bit of truth to power.

in such circumstances, means realizing the constraints on what you can do.

An example from Badaracco's book, drawing on real events but using composites: Soon after Rebecca Olson took over a hospital, the board's chairman informed her that an employee was about to file a sexual harassment complaint against the hospital's vice president of operations, Richard Millar, who had also been the board's inside candidate for the CEO position to which Olson had just been named. Instead of firing Millar immediately, or resigning because this potentially incendiary problem was not something she had signed on for, Olson spent the next two months orchestrating Millar's resignation. Badaracco highlights four key principles that guided the actions she took to avoid a public-relations disaster:

- SHE DIDN'T ASSUME SHE KNEW EVERYTHING. "To survive and succeed it is critical to be realistic and not exaggerate how much you really understand" about a situation, writes Badaracco.

- SHE EXPECTED TO BE SURPRISED BY EVENTS. In the words of Dwight Eisenhower, who oversaw the largest military invasion in history, "Rely on planning, but don't trust plans."

- SHE KEPT AN EYE ON THE INSIDERS. Olson had to proceed carefully in forcing Millar's resignation, because she was asking the hospital's inner circle to cast out one of its own.

- SHE TRUSTED, BUT SHE ALSO CUT THE CARDS.
Quiet leaders "give their trust carefully," writes
Badaracco, "and don't treat it like loose change."

Use Small Wins

During his tenure at a financial firm, Peter Grant (a pseudonym) maintained a strong commitment to hiring minorities. He "could have made a big public issue about his concerns," writes Meyerson, "but he believed that if he made any outright attempts to change recruiting policy or to challenge underlying assumptions, it might be threatening to his colleagues and might arouse a great deal of resistance." So whenever he hired solid minority candidates, he asked them to make a similar commitment to hiring people of color and to actively maintain their relationships with those hires. Thirty years later, Grant, now in the executive ranks, is "addressing issues of diversity much more actively and openly." The process he had started "with tiny steps decades ago had been responsible for the hiring of more than 3,500 minority employees."

Many management experts emphasize the motivational aspects of small wins, but Meyerson, a student of movement politics, homes in on its coalition-building benefits. "Grant kept his efforts to hire people of color out of the limelight until he'd built up a critical mass of success—and then he was able to call attention to it," she says. "Tempered radicals are really resourceful about amplifying and framing their small victories so as to add people and add talk to their work. Calling attention to the small win opens up the possibility of a conversation. It provokes questions, identifies resistance, uncovers unknown allies and information, and cultivates organizational wisdom by distinguishing between the things that we can change and the things that we can't."

For Further Reading

Tempered Radicals: How People Use Difference to Inspire Change at Work by Debra E. Meyerson (2001, Harvard Business School Press)

Leading Quietly: An Unorthodox Guide to Doing the Right Thing by Joseph L. Badaracco, Jr. (2002, Harvard Business School Press)

Reprint U0204C

New Leadership Role?

• • •

Michael Watkins

Every year thousands of managers make transitions into new jobs—more than 600,000 in the *Fortune* 500 alone. But there's little good advice on how you can take charge in a new leadership role. This is surprising, because the actions new leaders take during their first few months have a big impact on their success or failure. Transitions are times when organizations can be reshaped, in part because everybody is expecting a change. But they're also periods when new leaders are most vulnerable, because they lack detailed knowledge of the new role and haven't established new working relationships.

So what does it take to make a successful transition? Dan Ciampa and I have explored that question in dozens of interviews with experienced managers and in years of consulting work. We distilled the answers into a set of basic principles for taking charge. The single most important principle? *Get early wins to build momentum fast.* By the end of the first six months, the new leader must have begun to energize people and focus them on solving important business problems, in ways that have a quick, dramatic impact.

The key to an early win is to identify problems that (a) can be tackled in a reasonable period of time and (b) have solutions that will result in tangible operational and financial improvements. The new COO of a manufacturing company, for example, focused on the company's distribution system. Distributors were complaining about responsiveness. The executive could see that there were too many warehouses, and that the product traveled too long to get to the customer. By focusing a cross-functional team on streamlining the system he got some early wins, simultaneously reducing costs and increasing satisfaction among distributors.

To secure early wins, a new leader should:

- ESTABLISH A-ITEM PRIORITIES. These are major objectives that she must accomplish in the first couple of years. That lets her determine goals for the first few months in the context of these longer-term objectives. When she sets out to get some early wins, she can simultaneously move the organization toward the longer-term goals.

- IDENTIFY A CENTER OF GRAVITY. For our new COO it was the distribution system, but the right center of gravity depends on the business. In a pharmaceutical company it might be a key part of the drug discovery process; in an auto company, the handoff from product development to manufacturing. Regardless, the chosen center of gravity must be an area that is important and that allows for substantial performance improvement.

- INITIATE PILOT PROJECTS. These are specific initiatives within the center of gravity to secure early wins. Implementation plans for the projects should define the standards to be used, the resources needed, and the methodologies to be employed, while specifying both tangible and intangible goals.

How early wins are achieved also is important. Beyond tangible results, pilot projects should create *new models of behavior* consistent with the new leader's vision of how the organization should work. This means involving the right people, defining stretch goals, marshaling resources, setting deadlines, pushing for results, and then rewarding successes. Our new COO deliberately chose a cross-functional team because the company still worked largely in functional silos. The overarching goal is to set up a virtuous circle, building from modest early improvements to more fundamental ones in ways that reinforce desired behaviors.

At the same time, early wins must be achieved in ways that are *consistent with the culture* of the organization. In some businesses this means low-key collaboration; in others, high-profile, individually driven success. Whatever the case, the new leader must understand the culture well enough to recognize what will "count" as a win and what won't.

Finally, success in getting early wins is built on a *foundation of effective learning* early on. Because the new leader's situation is fraught with complexities and uncertainties, efficient learning during the transition is vital. Success in identifying where and how to take those early shots is a function not only of technical understanding, but also of insight into the culture and politics of the organization.

Reprint U9909E

Companies Don't Develop Leaders, CEOs Do

An Interview with Noel Tichy

●   ●   ●

Noel Tichy, professor of organizational behavior at the University of Michigan, is an author of *Control Your Destiny or Someone Else Will* (revised ed., HarperBusiness, 2001), the book on how GE manages. Tichy's other book, *The Leadership Engine: How Winning Companies Build Leaders at Every Level,* coauthored with Eli Cohen and published by HarperBusiness in 2002, profiles the tactics of leaders at GE, Compaq, Pepsi, Allied-Signal, ServiceMaster, Intel, and other companies. Although Tichy has long been a proponent of what is called action learning for managers—learning through participation in hands-on projects—*The Leadership Engine* focuses on the role of the CEO in leadership development.

Tichy argues that an organization's most developed leaders should be actively involved in the education and development of other leaders.

Tichy spoke to writer Tom Brown about how successful companies actually put the "leader" in "leadership development."

You assert that CEOs and other top executives should become in-house teachers. Why?

The field of management development has been dominated too long by consultants, professors, and corporate staff specialists. Given the context in which all businesses must operate these days—rapid globalization, vast technological changes, huge industrial transformations—the time is perfect for younger managers to be taught by people who have actually proven they can win battles in the marketplace.

Only a company with deep levels of leadership at all levels can steer confidently into the kind of continuous transformation facing most companies right now. The best people to groom such leadership are the corporate leaders who already have a proven track record of success.

This is by no means the norm. Why?

Many entrepreneurs—for example, a Bill Gates at Microsoft—have built huge companies that are, in essence, one-man shows. Such leaders often aren't interested in building leadership capacity in others, which will be regrettable in the long run. Of course, in many other companies, management bureaucrats still rule, even at the top. These executives are more interested in preserving their companies, not growing them.

I am fascinated by the group of elite leaders who see themselves as the primary stewards of human capital inside their companies. They define their job as primarily leaving a legacy of talent that can carry the company forward. They are Olympians in my mind, the "Michael Jordans" of the organizational world.

But you agree such leaders are not the norm?

These executives are perhaps 10% of the corporate population, if that. A Jack Welch, who did so well at GE, is still a maverick: Most companies would have killed off the careers of a young Welch. Companies that have stumbled badly of late—a General Motors or a Westinghouse— definitely had people like Welch in their ranks.

But in failing companies, a mentality that rewards behaviors that are conservative and risk-averse rules the day. It rewards people who don't rock the boat or resist harsh change. And this mentality will invariably punish or exile Welch types.

Thus, we need to know more about those companies in which such bold leadership prevails. And we need to know much more about how companies make such bold leadership a part of the institution—because they tend to do it by growing other maverick managers in-house.

The assumption here is that younger managers can learn from a wise and knowledgeable CEO. Is this true?

First, we need to emphasize that classroom learning is perhaps 20% of a leader's development. (This is so even if the classes are taught by CEOs.) Formal training, when embellished by myriad other development activities—from strategic planning sessions to annual goal setting—is the key. The strength of an Andy Grove at Intel is that this CEO has grown hundreds of other managers who share his base of competence.

Such leaders have leveraged themselves by having what I call a "teachable point of view": the ability to coalesce judgments about products, services, distribution channels, market dynamics, and all the other components of running a business, and the ability to cultivate that knowledge in less-experienced minds. The veteran leaders teach; their students grow by acting, doing, conducting business *after* receiving solid leadership guidance.

Perhaps the real "proof" that this approach fundamentally works is that investors in the capital markets have plainly been rewarding leaders like Intel's Grove—and have pushed to dump past CEOs at IBM, Kodak, American Express, and, just recently, Apple Computer, to name only a few.

Leaders must need to teach more than the basics of providing products and services.

Most definitely. The leaders we observed also taught about the values that would best align with and support business goals. They taught how to energize other people, even to energize to the scale of an entire organization. This is equally important training.

You say that "winning organizations build leaders at every level." What do you mean by "winning"?

I admire the simple definition of Larry Selden, who is a finance professor at Columbia University (retired). You can enhance his basic definition many ways, but one would be hard-pressed today to call a company that is not realizing a 16% return on assets and double-digit top-line revenue growth a winner.

In all the companies you've visited, are there two or three top things that leaders consistently do?

The leaders we studied came in different sizes, personalities, age levels, and personal backgrounds. But these leaders all understood that one leads when he or she accomplishes action through other people while also altering people's mindset and view of the world. The followers are being prepared to take over and lead by themselves.

Was there a common "syllabus" for the courses taught by different CEOs at different companies?

They stressed the essential lessons they have learned about running organizations. They stressed personal and organizational values. They taught the basics of creating or growing shareholder value (about which a lot of managers, even senior managers, are clueless). They taught how to compete. And they all talked about the importance of having positive emotion in an organization, creating a high level of energy and a keen edge.

How can an organization have an "edge"?

It's critical that leaders learn how to steer into tough decisions, to make decisions boldly and willingly, and be able to live with the consequences. Leaders must be able to see reality as it is, and able to act on what they see.

How much time can a CEO afford to spend teaching?

A leader like Larry Bossidy at Allied-Signal teaches all the time. Only a minor amount of his time is spent in a classroom setting. But he provides real-time feedback and coaching in contexts as diverse as strategy, business, and human resource reviews.

Bossidy writes letters to each key executive—three letters a year!—giving each one feedback, assessment, suggestions, and advice. He sends these after the strategic, operating, and human resource reviews. What else is this but teaching? So when I say that executives should be teachers, I'm not talking about them becoming stereo-typical professors.

Does this apply to all managers? Should first-line supervisors teach?

Absolutely. Look at the U.S. military and some of its special operating forces, such as the Navy Seals. These men and women are arguably the 48,000 best soldiers in the world. Dig deep into their training program and you'll find that the "teachers" holding sergeant rank are just as involved in developing leadership as the generals and admirals.

What kind of facilities does a company need to teach?

Many major corporations have done significant formal training out of rented hotel space. I think it says a lot when a company like General Electric spearheads its development commitment by allocating real estate as sub-stantial as Crotonville. But growing tomorrow's leaders is not a bricks-and-mortar issue. It's an involvement-from-the-top issue.

How does one prevent younger managers from being fearful of the leader as teacher?

You can't prevent a certain level of fear from entering such a process. Nor do you want to. I learned a lot when

I was part of a General Electric "Outward Bound" experience in the '80s. The instructor picked me first to scale a granite wall. I'm no rock climber; I gulped. Although I was always harnessed and safe, I thought, "I might die up there!"

A manager-student who must do a 90-day project to find new acquisition prospects as part of a CEO-led action-learning program is prone to the same kind of natural fear and anxiety. He has to stay up all night before the day he must present his learnings and conclusions. He starts to think, "My career might die tomorrow!" But research has shown that the right amount of anxiety and fear enhance learning, as long as it's not so much that paralysis sets in.

And, yes, any time a younger manager presents research, findings, or opinions to an accomplished leader, there's going to be a certain level of "grading" taking place. A CEO judges people first by what he sees.

You talk about "teachable moments." What are they, and why are they important?

It's critical that leaders condense their own career experience into those magical moments of personal transition—moments when something major happened to them and a major learning evolved from it. Such career (or life) transition points are teachable moments. Leaders need only extract the wisdom from such experiences, and pass it along.

So there's something to be said for the value of "stories" inside a company?

Yes. Stories have always been important in disciplines like religion for inculcating cultural values through the generations. The approach works in business as well.

Perhaps the point to make here is that, whether it be soft stories or hard business tactics, you can't have a learning organization unless it is first a teaching organization. When CEOs and other executives share their best experiental lessons from a teachable point of view, it's potent.

Your university career has been all about teaching. Your book is all about the need for leaders to teach. What about the old saw "Those who can, do. Those who can't, teach"?

Look at the companies we list in *The Leadership Engine*. Look at the successful, energetic leaders we profile. You will see strong evidence that those who can teach *should* teach. I'd even say they must.

Reprint U9710B

Neoteny

How Leaders Recruit the
Right Kind of Followers

•   •   •

Loren Gary

What motivates or inspires a follower? Is it the leader's charisma? Yes, to a significant extent, but our understanding of that term needs adjusting, says renowned leadership expert Warren G. Bennis. True charisma is not so much a set of innate traits as it is "the product of a social interaction." Indeed, so intertwined are follower and leader that the two roles "seem to be isomorphic," he observed in a recent interview. In other words, honing the skills of followership can help you become a good leader.

For their book, *Geeks and Geezers*, Bennis and coauthor Robert J. Thomas interviewed 43 noted organizational leaders; the geeks were all age 35 or younger, while the geezers were 70 or older. One of the most intriguing insights that emerged from their research was that the ability to transcend adversity and the knack for engaging others by creating shared meaning do not diminish with age. Every leader in the 70-and-over group "has one quality of overriding importance," they write: *neoteny,* a zoological term that Bennis and Thomas use to refer to "all those wonderful qualities that we associate with youth: curiosity, playfulness, eagerness, fearlessness, warmth, energy."

In nature, neoteny's hallmark is the ability of an infant to recruit a particular kind of follower: an engaged adult who will provide the care and nurture on which the infant depends for his or her survival. Because the term *neoteny* "gets at the interaction between leaders and followers," Bennis suggests that it's "a more useful term than charisma." A neotenic leader is able to recruit a particular kind of follower—what Robert E. Kelley refers to as an "exemplary follower" as opposed to a conformist. As he explains in *The Power of Followership,* exemplary followers are distinguished by the added value they bring to work that is crucial to the mission of the organization: they're always thinking about ways to be more useful.

By contrast, conformists may be actively engaged in the work assigned to them, but they don't exhibit much independent thinking. Overwhelmed by too many choices and too much uncertainty, they are all too willing to be swayed by the self-confident views and stirring pronouncements of the charismatic leader.

So what enables the neotenic leader to recruit independent-minded initiative-takers to the cause? The same skills that help you become an exemplary follower. Be a "first-class noticer," says Bennis, paraphrasing Saul Bellow's description of a character in his novel *Ravelstein*. This ability to recognize hidden significance, opportunities, and talent requires "a process orientation," says Harvard University psychologist Ellen J. Langer, author of the classic book *Mindfulness*. "People often confuse the stability of their mindsets with the stability of the phenomena they're observing," she explains.

> Charismatic leadership often creates conformists, but neotenic leadership elicits independent-minded followership.

"Most of us don't wake up to change until it's a big change that has occurred. If you only tune in when the situation becomes markedly different, then you tend to see things as being more still or stable than they are. But when you're mindful, you're aware that the situation is in flux." Instead of replaying old conversations in your head, you're alive to what is new in the current situation and to how contexts may have changed.

"It all depends on uncertainty," Langer continues. "Without it, people don't pay attention." This tolerance of uncertainty unites neotenic leaders and exemplary followers. Not only does the leader's mindful acknowledgement of how things can change cause followers to see that she's attuned to the present and therefore trustworthy, it also gives them encouragement. Followers see that their willingness to take initiative in uncertainty will be welcomed. And in exercising that initiative, they are developing their leadership skills.

For Further Reading

Geeks and Geezers: How Era, Values, and Defining Moments Shape Leaders by Warren G. Bennis and Robert J. Thomas (2002, Harvard Business School Press)

The Power of Followership: How to Create Leaders People Want to Follow and Followers Who Lead Themselves by Robert E. Kelley (1992, Doubleday Currency)

Mindfulness by Ellen J. Langer (1990, Perseus)

Reprint U0209D

Communicating
Effectively
About Change

* * *

Managers who can get their people on board demonstrate savvy communication skills. They know how to convey a compelling message about why change is valuable and how their people can turn an alluring vision of a better future into current, concrete reality. Once employees understand the importance of change and see a way to make it happen, they're more able to embrace and support the initiative driving the change.

In this section, you'll find an array of practical guidelines for communicating effectively about change—everything from conveying confidence and credibility to defining clear goals and selecting the right combination of communication channels. You'll also discover how to point your people's attention to the most important aspects of a change initiative, how to get subordinates "fired up" about change, and how to develop the emotional skills so essential for effective communication.

Start applying the strategies described in the articles in this final section, and you'll start taking huge strides toward building enthusiasm for change, creativity, and initiative in your team.

Effective
Leadership
Communications

* * *

John Baldoni

Two American Airlines planes were hijacked on September 11, 2001. The airline suffered another devastating blow two months later when one of its airliners crashed shortly after takeoff in Queens, N.Y. The company's CEO, Donald J. Carty, responded to this catastrophic loss by making a very deliberate effort to be visible both to his employees and to the public.

The usually reserved Carty, who normally doesn't seek the spotlight, was out front fielding questions from the media—he even took a turn on *Larry King Live* to demonstrate his company's resolve. After the crash in Queens, he traveled to New York to offer condolences to grieving flight attendants and gate agents. Carty is not without his critics; union leaders and rank-and-file employees believe he needs to be more communicative, especially about employee issues. American, like other airlines, laid off thousands of workers after September 11. But Carty has since instructed his management team to get out into the field to keep employees informed and boost their morale.

Carty and his team demonstrate leadership communications in action. Establishing effective leadership communications isn't a simple task, but it does boil down to following some fairly simple rules. Be consistent. Establish clear goals. Set a good example. Emphasize that everyone, across the company, needs to communicate effectively.

Too often, leadership communications is seen as the sole purview of public affairs or marketing people. It isn't; it's central to the real business of leaders throughout an organization. The presence of leaders, actively communicating, is key, not just in times of challenge, but in the ongoing efforts to keep a company's vision clearly focused for customers and employees alike.

Richard Teerlink revitalized Harley-Davidson through frequent and relentless communications with dealers and owners. Herb Kelleher was a veritable communications dynamo for Southwest Airlines, traveling coach to learn about the state of the business from his frontline employees. And Steve Jobs, CEO of Apple Computer, has been key to the company's turnaround by acting as a visionary architect who keeps employees and customers energized and loyal.

"A brilliant strategy doesn't work unless everyone understands and believes in it. That takes communication," says Chuck Snearly, director of stakeholder communications for Ford Motor Company. "Employees of the most effective organizations trust their leaders and have a sense of purpose and belonging. Virtually any duty that you can identify for a leader has a communications element attached to it."

Giving a Voice to Leadership

A leadership communication is a message of significant importance that flows from the leader to key stakeholders—employees, customers, investors, even the public at large. This message may come in an e-mail, a one on-one conversation, or a speech to thousands.

A message from the CEO about where she wants to take the organization in the future is a leadership communication. A memo from the CEO rescheduling a meeting is not. Leadership communications are rooted in the culture and values of the organization, and they pertain to vision, mission, transformation, and calls to action. These messages may be directed at an individual, a team, or an entire organization. Their purpose is straightforward: to establish, or continue to build, trust between leader and follower.

It is a natural tendency to look inward and retreat during times of crisis, but the examples just mentioned demonstrate that the natural tendency may not be the right reaction. Better to get out front with the truth than to dissemble behind public relations fronts.

"Communication is the backbone of leadership," says Don Duffy, an executive producer with Williams/Gerard, a leading corporate communications firm. "People need direction and leadership, and without constant communication you have no leadership."

Impact on the Culture

Walk into a place with healthy open communications and you find people energized and alive. They have a sense of purpose and know where they are going, in part because they have a leader who has told them. Just the opposite occurs with ineffective communications. People are drawn into themselves and seem fearful. And no wonder. They likely do not know what to expect next—no one has told them.

"If people from the top to the bottom of your organization don't understand your strategy, then you don't have one," says Dr. Daniel Denison, professor of management and organization at the International Institute for Management Development (IMD) in Lausanne, Switzerland, and principal of Denison Consulting in Ann Arbor, Michigan. "You may have a mission, a vision, or a business plan, but without alignment and understanding across levels, no one can implement a business strategy."

Denison has spent the past two decades doing research on how corporate culture and leadership are linked to bottom-line performance. "It's amazing how much time corporations spend articulating the CEO's values and vision and how little time they spend trying to understand if anyone got the message."

"Executives who are great strategists and think that implementation is a 'no-brainer' often end up destroying alignment instead of building the tight integration that they need from top to bottom," adds Denison. "That kind of management philosophy ends up separating thinkers from doers by putting those who think at the top and those who do everywhere else. In order for an organization to succeed, you need thinkers and doers at all levels."

Leadership messages reflect organizational culture and values, but they also require the leader's personal commitment. The leader endorses the culture by communicating what is beneficial for the organization and the people in it. In other words, the leader links the macro picture—what's good for everybody—with the micro picture—what's in it for each listener. As such, these leadership messages are designed to gain commitment from employees and create a bond of trust between leader and follower.

Today's challenging business environment demands leadership messages. "The slower the business, the more you need to communicate," says Duffy. "When business is slow, employees will have more time to communicate with one another. You can influence that conversation by communicating regularly, or you can let them speculate on what you should be telling them!" People want their leaders to be frank and honest and at the same time provide guidance and direction.

How to Initiate Communication

Here are some steps you can take to initiate effective leadership communications.

Be Consistent

Consistency of message is essential. Detractors said Ronald Reagan gave only one speech—the same one over and over again. Former British Prime Minister Margaret Thatcher, an admirer, said that while it may have been true that Reagan had only "five or six" ideas, those he had were "big ones." Business leaders, too, need to continually reinforce their big ideas in conjunction with the core values of their organization so that key stakeholders understand what the enterprise stands for.

Denison believes communicators have a tough, but necessary, job. "The challenge for communicators is to build vitality through repetition." Alignment of vision, values, and objectives depends on the quality and frequency of the message.

Ford's Snearly, who spends his days invigorating and reinvigorating corporate messages, agrees. "In a large organization, repetition helps spread the word," he says. "It is a mistake for senior leaders to assume that their direct reports will pass along the right message to their direct reports, and so on down the line. In small and large organizations alike, even after the message has been completely disseminated, repetition helps everyone stay focused on the strategy and goals. On a rational level, repetition helps everyone understand what they are supposed to do. On an emotional level, it reinforces the human need to bond and be a part of a group."

Set Clear, Credible Targets

Tell your people where you want to take the organization. Steve Jobs, for example, uses his vision statements to encourage people to think about the future and stay focused on new products.

Gain Commitment from Key Stakeholders

Engage the hearts and minds of your people. Excite them with the possibilities and then ask for their commitment. And get your people to commit to the details: What they will do and when and how. General Peter Pace of the U.S. Marines once reported to six different people. Pace strove to keep all his superiors fully informed. When disagreements arose, as Michael Useem notes in *Leading Up,* Pace spoke his mind but never went behind any of his superiors' backs.

Pace did not always get the commitments he wanted, but he felt that his transparent communications style served him, his superiors, and the 92,000 Marines under his command well.

Coach, Coach, Coach

So much of leadership is about accomplishing results through others. This is where leadership communications plays a vital role. Your people can succeed only if they have the necessary tools and resources—as well as your personal involvement. Always provide plenty of feedback. Many senior leaders make it a habit to coach their direct reports regularly, dispensing praise as well as advice on improvement week by week, rather than waiting until the annual performance review to give actionable feedback.

Be Out Front

As the project or the enterprise moves forward (or even backward), make certain you are front and center helping to steer. See and be seen—as well as heard. Don Carty of American Airlines is a shining example of this; his company is under siege, but he's out front taking the heat.

Issue Calls to Action

Need to change direction in the face of unforeseen circumstances? Or need to spur the team along? Speak up and ask for their support. Telling people what needs to be done and by whom is not micromanagement; it's leadership. Football coaches excel at this: Let's run our game plan, get our points, and go home with a victory.

Emphasize That Everyone Needs to Communicate Effectively

Leaders aren't the only ones who need to communicate. Employees need to foster communication skills peer-to-peer as well as up and down the organizational ladder. If only leaders speak, the organization as a whole is silent. Teams, departments, and even entire organizations that emphasize communications seem to have a greater sense of purpose and unity. Why? Because people take the time to keep one another informed.

Choose the Media Wisely

Leaders need to be sensitive to the media they utilize. Good advice can be dispensed through the keyboard, but electronic media should not supplant face-to-face communications, especially when comments about performance are being delivered. E-mail is fine for announcements or for clarifications of ongoing communications,

How the British Bulldog
Made Himself Heard

One of the greatest leaders—and communicators—of the twentieth century didn't begin that way. Plagued with a stutter early in life, Winston Churchill determined to rise above his mother's advice that he pick a career that didn't involve public speaking. Rise above it he did, and his rules for success in communicating with an audience were few but seminal:

1. **Get their attention.** Communication is two-way. You can't communicate with your listeners if they're not listening. You must begin by grabbing their attention powerfully.
2. **Repeat regularly.** Churchill was known for having a few principles and tirelessly repeating them. There's nothing like artful repetition to make sure a message gets across.
3. **Bring language to life.** Churchill well understood the importance of variety in tone, speed, language, and emphasis to hold the audience's attention. He paid particular attention to verbs in public

but it is inappropriate for one-on-one communications, e.g., a coaching session. It is, however, OK to use e-mail to supplement a coaching session.

Large-scale meetings are ideal for generating excitement about the company's vision and mission and for com-

speaking, knowing that verbs make language come alive.

4. **End powerfully.** People remember the last thing you've said, so make it good. Save some of your best stuff for your close.

5. **Use simple gestures.** A study of videos of Churchill's speeches shows a man who stood squarely, usually with one hand grasping his lapel or resting firmly on his hip. The other arm occasionally comes forward to make a strong vertical gesture emphasizing a point he's making. His arms never "windmill" around his body; the effect of that is to undercut the strength and dignity of the speaker.

6. **Pause.** One of the longest pauses ever recorded in a political speech came in an address Churchill made to the Canadian Parliament in 1941. Churchill had been told that England would "have her neck wrung like a chicken." His riposte to this threat? "Some chicken. [Pause.] Some neck." Churchill confidently waited for the laughter and applause to end before uttering the next phrase. It's a classic moment of oratory.

municating an urgent need for change. Ideally, leaders should speak from the heart about where they want the organization to go. Presentations may be scripted in advance, but speakers should try to work from notes, making as much eye contact as possible.

You can likely think of many more examples yourself—these are just for starters.

Enable Listening

Effective leadership communications is not a one-way stream of messages from top to bottom; messages must flow uphill, too. If employees are to feel they have a stake in the organization and its mission, it is absolutely critical for the leader to facilitate two-way communication, specifically allowing feedback in the form of ideas, suggestions, and even dissent. The ownership stake is initiated, nurtured, augmented, tested, and fulfilled through leadership communications.

By encountering the leadership message over and over again, and in many different circumstances, employees come to a better understanding of what the leader wants, what the organization needs, and how they fit into the picture. In time, leader and follower form a solidarity rooted in mutual respect. When that occurs, leader and follower can pursue organizational goals united in purpose and bonded in mutual trust.

For Further Reading

Leading Up: How to Lead Your Boss So You Both Win by Michael Useem (2001, Crown Business/Random House)

Reprint C0204A

Making an Impact

• • •

David Stauffer

Bill Clinton has it. Colin Powell does, too. And Pope John Paul II. Princess Diana had it big time, as did President Kennedy.

"It" is a combination of appearance, stature, and bearing that sends almost instantaneous positive signals to others. People who have examined immediate personal impact say "it" isn't size, height, or even physical beauty—although endowments in these areas can contribute to it. Nor is it extroversion or other aspects of personality—although, again, they can contribute.

No, the "it" at issue here is something else. "In Hollywood, it's called star quality," says executive coach James B. Anderson, president of the Anderson Leadership Group in Vienna, Virginia. "In the military, it's command presence. Whatever it's called, it comes from attitude, from focus, and from self-assurance."

Author and personal presentation expert Tony Alessandra asks, "Have you ever seen someone walk into a room and cause all eyes to turn, admiringly, in his or her direction? This is because he or she conveys positive silent messages. They are sent by the way you carry yourself physically, emotionally, and intellectually."

> Just before you enter a room, pick up your shoulders and roll them back and down. When you're standing, place your feet approximately shoulder-width apart.

Fortunately, the ability to send silent messages that make an immediate positive impression on others is available and accessible to all of us. Here are seven suggestions for enhancing what you communicate to others on first sight.

1: Develop a Positive Outlook

You're at a considerable disadvantage if you hope to send out positive vibes when your own outlook is negative or neutral. "The optimistic person is more likely to appear energetic and engaged, to be smiling, and to maintain eye contact with others," says Alessandra. That's reasonable; but even if you don't have the relentlessly joyous air of a Roberto Benigni, try at least to take a favorable view of the meeting, reception, or other event at hand. Before you walk in the room, envision something good you might get from the occasion—being introduced to an important new contact, for example, or making a good impression on the chairman you'd like to work for.

Afterward, work on your longer-term outlook. For example: "Consciously do at least one thing every day for someone else, something totally without ulterior motive, from which you stand to gain nothing," suggests Camille Lavington, an executive coach who describes her speciality as executive enhancement. "The great feeling you derive from this will amaze you—and will be reflected in the way you look on first sight to others."

2: Get "Outside" Yourself

If you go into any interpersonal encounter with your mind even partially focused on your own concerns, you make it just about impossible to have a favorable instant effect on others. Those self-concerns can range from the immediate ("Has my mousse still got my cowlick pinned down?") to the overarching ("If the bull market lasts, maybe I won't need Social Security"). Either way, you appear closed rather than open. Think how readily *you* can spot someone whose mind is somewhere else.

In this case, take the situational cure offered by author and speaker Sam Horn, president of Action Seminars. "Focus your attention on others," she advises, "by giving 'em 'L'—the following four-L technique: *Look* at others with interest. *Lean* forward slightly, as though to catch every word. *Lift* your eyebrows. *Level* your approach—by sitting with others who are sitting and standing with those who are standing. With the four-Ls, you project an interest in others that attracts them to you."

Here, too, you're well served by a longer-term strategy, which essentially consists of getting more involved in what's going on around you. In the self-improvement arena, that consists of developing the senses and skills that put you in closer touch with everything external: improving your listening skills and powers of observation, for example, or taking a class in any creative art, such as photography, silk-screening, or bird watching. Going even farther from the self, almost any worthwhile volunteer activity, from church and PTA to unpaid archeological digging on other continents, can't help but direct your focus outward.

3: Smile

"It's hard for anyone to resist a genuine smile," Horn says. *Genuine* is very important, she adds. "A smile you force to cover an internal focus on your fears will look forced. That's why you have to change your focus from yourself to others."

4: Exercise and Eat Right

If it seems as though you can't get away from the imperative to exercise in any sort of self-improvement effort these days, you're on target. Alessandra contends that, "People who are physically fit have a bounce in their step and a vibrancy in complexion that can unquestionably appeal to others." He says that diet counts, too. "Most of us realize either energy gains or impairment from eating certain kinds of foods. The trick is for each of us to discover those effects and ensure we eat for optimal energy when we're going to be with others."

If you already know, as so many time-crunched folks do, that a regimen of regular workouts isn't going to make your dance card until you're drawing a pension, you can at least give yourself a stature boost. It's suggested by David T. Bernhardt, associate professor of pediatrics and sports medicine at the University of Wisconsin Medical School, who notes, "Many of the things we do regularly tend to make us appear round-shouldered and slumped. Students slouch in chairs, while many office workers do the same in front of computer screens or in seemingly endless meetings. These things work against an immediately appealing appearance—an erect posture with our shoulders drawn back. You can develop this with exercises that develop the shoulder and back muscles." The easiest: Tape two tennis balls together, place them at your upper back between the shoulder blades, and press them against a wall. Then repeatedly pinch them between your shoulder blades. Do this for five to 10 minutes daily.

> *Look* at others with interest. *Lean* forward slightly, as though to catch every word. *Lift* your eyebrows. *Level* your approach—by sitting with others who are sitting and standing with those who are standing.

And take Horn's advice to be towering, not cowering. "Just before you enter a room, pick up your shoulders and roll them back and down. When you're standing, place your feet approximately shoulder-width apart. This is a more athletic, versus timid, stance. It's a way to appear confident—even when you aren't."

5: Know Your Goals

Can having a direction in life give you the appearance of having a direction in business and social interactions? Alessandra, for one, thinks it can. To illustrate, he tells of a little girl who told her kindergarten teacher she was drawing a picture of God. Informed by the teacher that "no one knows what God looks like," the student replied, "They will in a minute!" Like the little girl, Alessandra asserts, appealing people "possess a childlike faith in their vision; they truly believe they can create change. . . . People who have no vision or goals are meandering and can appear to be somehow out of place, rather than in and of the moment. Those who have defined their personal goals, on the other hand, may gain a visible measure of enthusiasm and self-confidence."

6: Forget Talk; Be Ready to Listen

Perhaps the single most common thought occupying the minds of people going into an interpersonal interaction is, "What will I say?" That's a double blow under the circumstances. It's a worry that may visibly show (see Step 2), and it could much more productively be flipped to put the pressure to perform on everyone else: "What will *they* say?"

"When you're completely receptive to others, rather than focused on yourself, you'll feel yourself relaxing,"

Don't Forget to Say Something Brilliant, Too

Even as you're practicing your confident stance and your four-L technique, and listening to everyone else while keeping your own goals firmly in mind, you need to remember that the most important part of making a strong impression on other people is having something worthwhile to say. Many presentation coaches leave you with the impression that content does not matter, that it's only about looking good, but nothing could be further from the truth. Your listeners may not remember everything you say, but they do remember the high points, and they are pretty shrewd about checking what you say against the unspoken signals you send out. This argues for making your attitude and message consistent. It also suggests that your message should be as simple and clear as possible. Here are four tips for maximizing the impact of what you have to say.

Connect with Your Core Beliefs

Are you nervous? Your listeners will pick up on that by noting all the little nonverbal signals: rapid eye scanning, shifting feet, shoulders that "bob and weave," sweaty palms, nervous swallowing. All these will suggest to the people whom you meet that you have something else besides what you're saying on your mind. Research suggests that people whose eyes shift a great deal are probably lying, so those listeners are right to be concerned. A good way to minimize nervousness is to make sure that what you're saying closely connects with ideas and beliefs that you're passionate about. The further we stray from our core beliefs, the more likely we are to telegraph uncertainty.

Tell Us Clearly How You Feel

You will increase your listeners' interest in what you have to say—as well as your own comfort level—if you become practiced at letting them know how you feel. Do you love the way the business is going right now, or do you hate it? What about that latest product launch—was it fabulous, or was it a turkey? Are you excited about the pending IPO? Don't leave your listeners in any doubt about your attitude on important issues. But do it with tact. Avoid the "emotional bull in the china shop" syndrome of people who bray their own opinions without being willing to listen to those of others.

Use Colorful Language

The art of good conversation has become so devalued that when we do meet someone who can express forcefully and elegantly what's on her mind, we cannot help but be impressed. We all think of clever things we wish we had said once the encounter is over; that's inevitable. The point is not to try to prepare memorable one-liners, but to be clear and strong about issues that are important to you. Successful use of "colorful language" will follow inevitably from passionate commitment to the topic at hand. Look constantly for ways to raise the verbal ante with metaphor: Don't say, "it made us a little upset," but rather, "it hit us like the proverbial runaway train."

Finish Your Sentences, and Let Others Finish Theirs

Our conversational life has fallen victim to our fast-paced, fractured lifestyle. The result is that we rarely finish what we begin. But if our listeners become used to hearing fragments, they will give us only fragmentary attention. Train yourself to speak in brief, complete thoughts. Hear others out. The impact on how closely you're listened to will be surprisingly large.

Horn says. "That's because the pressure is off; the people around us are our whole world at that moment." More important, that's the stealth weapon in your arsenal of assets that prompts others to form favorable immediate impressions of you. Almost everyone wants to feel important, to relate to others the worthwhile things he or she is doing—in other words, to be listened to.

7: Be Yourself

All of the foregoing advice notwithstanding, you're more likely to be an instant hit with others if you don't walk into gatherings with your head filled with other people's dos and don'ts. Which is not to say that you should discard Steps 1 through 6, but, rather, that you should take them one at a time and work to internalize them, so you make each in turn your default behavior.

Be wary of anyone's laundry list of ways to charm the socks off others. Executive coach Jim Anderson warns, "Some people who call themselves image consultants or something similar teach people, in effect, to be phonies. Don't feel that you have to be someone other than who you are. Instead, dare to be real—to be yourself. You want to figuratively say to others, 'If you aren't going to like me, I want you to dislike the way I really am, not the way I've been made by someone else.' You'll be more comfortable with yourself and more human and likable to others."

Horn offers similar advice as a guard against having the uncomfortable look of the person who has something to prove. "When we feel we have to prove to others how witty or smart we are, we appear to have a lack of ease. An appealing appearance comes from having nothing to prove."

For Further Reading

Charisma: Seven Keys to Developing the Magnetism That Leads to Success by Tony Alessandra (1998, Warner Books)

Concrete Confidence: A 30-Day Program for an Unshakable Foundation of Self-Assurance by Sam Horn (1997, St. Martin's Press)

You've Only Got Three Seconds: How to Make the Right Impression in Your Business and Social Life by Camille Lavington with Stephanie Losee (1998, Doubleday)

Reprint C9908B

Framing for Leadership

• • •

Melissa Raffoni

A manager's job is, quite simply, to motivate people toward achieving a common goal. Succeeding at this job requires a gamut of communication skills, ranging from delivering a prepared talk to helping team members negotiate the best way to move ahead on a project. No communication skill, however, is more critical to the manager than the ability to frame an issue effectively.

What exactly does it mean to "frame" or "reframe" an issue? Think about the metaphor behind the concept. A frame focuses attention on the painting it surrounds. Moreover, different frames draw out different aspects of the work. Putting a painting in a red frame brings out the red in the work; putting the same painting in a blue frame brings out the blue.

How someone frames an issue influences how others see it and focuses their attention on particular aspects of it; framing is the essence of targeting a communication to a specific audience.

> Framing represents the strategic part of communication.

Although the concept of framing seems quite rudimentary, the reality is that most people cannot do it well. This can especially be a problem for a manager leading a diverse, diversely talented team. Individuals tend to focus on their own particular needs and on matters relating to their specific areas of expertise; this is only natural. But in so doing, they may lose sight of the details that matter for the project they are currently working on.

For example, consider a multidisciplinary team that comes together to discuss how to improve a poor customer service rating. The conversation wanders from product development, to pricing, to internal political struggles. Although discussion of each of these topics is fruitful to some degree, the team is not making much progress at finding a solution to the problem.

This is where the manager steps in to reframe the discussion. He points out what is and isn't relevant to the issue at hand and brings the team back on track while simultaneously reassuring everyone that he hears and understands their concerns. By reframing the issue, he brings clarity to complexity.

Circumvent Obstacles

Helping employees get around roadblocks is one of the manager's most important roles. Even if she does a terrific job of communicating her vision and motivating others to work toward realizing it, her team will encounter obstacles. The best leaders anticipate what they will be and use framing techniques to help employees navigate around them.

They begin by isolating the issue and framing it so everyone understands it and its relevance to his or her work. Then, they highlight the options for removing the obstacles either by directly recommending courses of action or by posing questions that guide others to find them.

The manager's reframing ensures that everyone understands the issue at hand: "So, you are saying that we should lower the price." It incorporates the perspectives of the various audiences affected: "If we lower the price, customers will buy more, but we will lose margin and it will mean more work for marketing and sales. Do we still think this is the best option?" If the discussion gets off track, the manager uses reframing to bring everyone back to the issue: "Let's keep in mind that the question is whether or not we need to lower our price." The leader will continue to reframe the issue until the best solution emerges and the obstacle is removed.

Sometimes the obstacle is something employees are not comfortable discussing—for example, a colleague whose contributions are not hitting the mark. By framing tough questions in nonthreatening ways, managers can fix the problem and get everyone moving ahead: "Let's figure out what we need to do to make the project successful; do we need to move Jane to another project?"

Correct Organizational Disconnects

Strong leaders see where people need to come together. Because they typically oversee a group of people possessing different talents and skills, they are best positioned to point people to each other: "Your plan seems to be on track. You should consider setting up a meeting with marketing to make sure you are in synch. I know they are working to make your project a success but it might be helpful to review things with them, one more time, to make sure both departments are clear."

In this scenario, the leader frames the issue in a way that puts both parties in a positive light and makes it in the best interest of both to connect.

Change the Style, Change the Frame

In their book, *Primal Leadership* (Harvard Business School Press, 2002), Daniel Goleman, Richard Boyatzis, and Annie McKee state that the best leaders act according to one or more of six distinct approaches to leadership: visionary, coaching, affiliative, democratic, pacesetting, and commanding. Their research found that the leaders who achieve the best results practice more than one style on any given day, depending on business needs.

Skillful framing shapes a manager's communication to reflect the leadership style she needs for a particular situation. Strong leaders are cognizant of the role they want to play at any given time, and frame their communications accordingly.

Consider the following situation: a team is frustrated with the performance of a newly launched product and wants to discontinue it.

The manager can help the team in a variety of ways. She can decide that her purpose is to lift morale and convince the team to stay the course. By framing a discussion around the mission of the company and how this product is critical in achieving it, she assumes a visionary role. Or she might choose to drive the team to come together to brainstorm ways to improve the product, acting as a coach.

Which Frame When?

Framing represents the strategic part of communication and as such is critical to get right. In giving a presentation, people tend to focus on their delivery: Did they maintain eye contact? Were they too soft-spoken, or did they stumble over their words? While these aspects are important, they tend not to be the most important drivers of a communication's effectiveness.

Even the most eloquent of speakers can miss the mark if his communication is not framed to meet the audience's needs.

Before they speak, effective managers always have a specific purpose in mind. In some cases it may be to motivate or persuade; in other cases, it may be to transfer knowledge or drive consensus. Regardless, the purpose is clear and they will reframe their communications until they have met their objective.

Before every communication, ask yourself the following questions:

- What is the purpose of my communication?

- What do I want the listener to think, feel, or do after hearing my words?

131

- Have I incorporated what I know about the audience's perspective?

- How will my messages impact them?

- Have I answered the question "What's in it for me?"?

- What other aspects of the context are shaping the way people think, such as the culture or the severity of the issue?

- How credible am I in the eyes of the beholder?

- How can I frame what I say so as to increase my credibility?

Effective framing can be learned and strengthened with discipline and effort. The real challenge is when you are faced with the unexpected, such as new information or an unforeseen question. Keep your purpose and your audience top of mind, so you can thoughtfully frame a response that furthers your goals and strengthens your leadership.

Reprint C0212B

How to Get People on Board

• • •

Once upon a time there was such a thing as *business as usual*. Occasionally a company would embark on a change initiative, but when the initiative was over it was back to good old B.A.U. Alas, that was then and this is now. A large company today typically has dozens of initiatives in process simultaneously. It's also likely to be merging or acquiring, experimenting with e-business, and trying hard to develop new products or enter new markets. Business as usual? Right now it's all change, all the time.

The result: For managers, helping employees get with the (new) program—and helping them cope with uncertainty about the future—is almost a full-time occupation. Fortunately, this is a challenge that people who

specialize in change management have learned something about.

Sources of Anxiety

There are three big concerns in any time of change, says
Peter Thies, senior director with Delta Consulting Group.
Employees worry about issues related to:

1. WHAT THE FUTURE WILL BRING. "People are asking
   themselves things like, 'Will I be better off than I
   was before? Will I be able to be successful? Who's
   in charge of my career, my future?'" says Thies.

2. WHAT TO DO RIGHT NOW. Employees wonder what
   to tell family, peers, and staff about what's going
   on. They wonder how they themselves should
   react to the change.

3. WHETHER THE WHOLE THING IS MANAGEABLE. "It's
   questions like, 'Can we keep the wheels on while
   we're making this change?'" says Thies.

These worries may or may not be expressed directly,
but you can bet they'll be the subject of lunchtime conversations. "It's the 'coffee shop anxiety' that will drive
productivity down and lead your key talent to walk out
the door," says Kathryn Yates, a senior consultant with
Hewitt Associates. "It's very personal. And the manager

is the key to addressing those 'me' questions that get in the way of successfully implementing change."

What Managers Can Do

Managers charged with leading change know they have to communicate with employees, so they dutifully distribute informational memos and put on PowerPoint presentations. Those methods convey information—they tell employees what's in the works—but they rarely allay anxieties or help people get fired up about future prospects. For that to happen, say experienced change consultants, you need a different approach entirely.

Tap into Positive Emotions

Any high-performing company creates a strong emotional bond with its employees, argues Jon R. Katzenbach, whose book *Peak Performance: Aligning the Hearts and Minds of Your Employees* (Harvard Business School Press, 2000) describes five different strategies for building emotional commitment. And in a time of change, positive emotions are often the best antidote to feelings such as anxiety and powerlessness. The manager's task: Connect the change with objectives that employees care about. "Identify the emotional hot buttons in the group—what your people are going to respond to and develop some feeling about," advises Katzenbach.

Hot buttons are different, of course, for different people. Techies get excited about the feeling that they're out on the bleeding edge doing cool stuff. Salespeople and other competitors like the idea of winning in the marketplace. (Katzenbach: "If you have an aggressive competitor, make an enemy out of it and fight the enemy.") Employees in organizations such as Home Depot and Marriott are hired because they care about delivering great service. Depending on the context, you may be able to get people fired up about any of these objectives—or about others, such as the chance to earn a fat bonus or learn new skills. The key words: fired up. "They have to feel there's something more here than simply earning more money for shareholders," says Katzenbach.

Manage One-to-One

When Corning Cable Systems was about to undergo a major corporate restructuring, CEO Sandy Lyons began the process by holding individual meetings with some 50 top managers. The purpose? "To get them thinking, 'this is possible' and 'I have a say in it,'" says Lyons. It's no different if you have 5 direct reports rather than 50: Each person wants to know what's being planned and what it means for him or her—and most will want a chance to put in their two cents. "You have to be open, you have to engage people, and you have to empower them to be part of the solution," says Lyons.

One-to-one management in this context can utilize a variety of tools. For example, many companies conduct

Managing Change? Tap the Web.

Effective communication in a time of rapid change is two-way, not one-way. During Corning Cable Systems' restructuring, says president and CEO Sandy Lyons, "we put in a closed-loop intranet site. It talked about all the things that were part of the change. And anybody could go to that network and post a question. Within 48 hours there'd be an answer posted back.

"A lot of anxiety goes away when people get answers to questions."

employee surveys when change is afoot—and many survey results seem to vanish into a black hole so far as the employees are concerned. Charles Schwab, however, not only published the results of one such survey, it trained managers to analyze individual responses, says Tom Davenport, a principal with Towers Perrin's San Francisco office. Managers then sat down with employees to discuss responses. "They took employees through exercises to help them decide what to do about the responses they gave—what was underlying their concerns and how to respond to those issues."

Lead, Don't Force

"Most change initiatives are forced into organizations," says Chris Turner, a Xerox veteran who is author of *All Hat and No Cattle: Tales of a Corporate Outlaw* (Perseus Books, 2000). But force rarely works; even if people act as they're supposed to, they'll lack enthusiasm. Better, says Turner, to invite people to join in creating the change—and then to work first with the 25% or so who are likely to respond.

Leadership may also involve challenging the organization to live up to its stated objectives. "If the company wants more entrepreneurship but the pay structures don't encourage entrepreneurial behavior," says Turner, "then the manager's role is to say, 'Look, our current systems aren't encouraging this. We need to redesign the way we pay people.' The manager's role is to create the environment that fosters the kind of behaviors you want—and to understand what dissonances there are in the current system."

Reprint U0006A

Becoming a Resonant Leader

• • •

Loren Gary

Everywhere she turns, people are asking for a different kind of leadership, says Ginger Graham, group chairman of the medical products firm Guidant. The emotional repercussions of world events and the precarious situations of many companies have altered the demands placed on her.

Shareholders and analysts used to insist that she be able "to spin the future—to talk about being the first and the coolest," Graham says. Otherwise, "your P/E ratios would be lower and your market cap wouldn't move much. But selling futures isn't very cool right now—underpromising and overdelivering and having solid fundamentals are." Employees want some assurance that there'll be a future at all. After the debacles at Enron and Global Crossing, they need their leaders to function as emotional shock absorbers. "They also require a different level of discussion and disclosure" about the workings of such things as Guidant's 401(k) and defined-contribution retirement plans. "And they want to know more about you the leader," adds Graham. "They want you to be available at a different level because they're searching."

Employees are asking that leaders act with greater integrity and be more emotionally available—at the very time that leaders, fighting for their organizations' survival, are asking employees to accept painful losses. So not only have the past year's startling examples of institutional fragility raised people's expectations, they've also heightened leaders' sense of vulnerability. These events have strained leaders' ability to maintain the distinction between self and role, says Ronald A. Heifetz, founding director of the Center for Public Leadership at Harvard's John F. Kennedy School of Government.

Leaders must engage in what Heifetz calls *adaptive work*—meeting an ongoing stream of challenges that simultaneously represent dangers and opportunities, and asking in the face of each, "What here is worth conserving and what do we need to let go of in order to thrive in the new environment?" This puts leaders in the line of fire, perhaps in ways they've never experienced. "If you don't like bad news, you should get out of the leadership business," observes Kim Campbell, Canada's first female prime minister and Lecturer in Public Policy at the Kennedy School of Government. "Your job is to hear as much bad news as there is out there and to figure out ways of dealing with it."

"Whenever a company faces a shock, how the leadership handles its own emotions can determine whether the company survives," says Daniel Goleman, coauthor of *Primal Leadership*. Leaders' emotional intelligence (EI)—their ability to manage their own and others' emotions in ways that drive business performance—thus provides the key to success. Training that boosts EI and stratagems for enhancing leadership teams' adaptive capacity can make all the difference.

An EI Primer

"Emotions are contagious," says Goleman. "Research shows that they determine 50% to 70% of the workplace climate; that climate, in turn, determines 20% to 30% of a company's performance." What's more, EI accounts for 85% of what distinguishes the stars in top leadership positions from low-level performers.

What Goleman and coauthors Richard Boyatzis and Annie McKee call *resonant leadership*—the ability to articulate a group's shared yet unexpressed feelings and to give voice to a mission that inspires others—is a function of four basic EI competencies:

- SELF-AWARENESS—the ability to read your own emotions and accurately assess your personality.

- SELF-MANAGEMENT—the ability to keep disruptive emotions under control and to be trustworthy, flexible, and optimistic.

- SOCIAL AWARENESS—the ability to empathize with others' concerns.

- RELATIONSHIP MANAGEMENT—the ability to inspire, persuade, and resolve disagreements.

The problem is, the higher up in an organization you are, the more inflated your assessment of your own EI skills. "So why don't more top leaders solicit and encourage accurate feedback?" Goleman and his coauthors ask. "It's often because they truly believe that they can't change." Yet there is compelling evidence that suggests otherwise.

Most training programs that seek to develop EI and leadership skills fail because they target the neocortex, the part of the brain that governs analytical and technical ability, rather than the limbic system, which controls feelings, impulses, and desires. The limbic brain "is a much slower learner—particularly when the challenge is to relearn deeply ingrained habits," write Goleman et al. But when "the right model is used, training can actually alter the brain centers that regulate negative and positive emotions," creating long-term EI skill improvements. The key is *self-directed learning* "intentionally developing or strengthening an aspect of who you are or who you want to be, or both." This process involves five phases of discovery:

1. UNCOVERING your ideal self—who you want to be.

2. FIGURING OUT who you actually are and where your strengths and weaknesses lie.

3. CREATING a learning agenda for building on your strengths while filling in the gaps.

4. EXPERIMENTING with and practicing new behaviors, thoughts, and feelings to the point of mastery.

5. DEVELOPING supportive and trusting relationships that make change possible.

Groupthink and the Glass Ceiling

As expectations get ratcheted up, even emotionally intelligent leaders can fall prey to a kind of bunker mentality. The leadership team "starts talking more to itself than to frontline workers and customers," says Darrell Rigby, a director of the management consulting firm Bain & Co. "Disagreement becomes viewed as disloyalty." One way to counteract this tendency toward groupthink is to make sure your leadership team comprises diverse styles and perspectives. Sometimes, insisting on gender and ethnic diversity is the only way to ensure that a team considers a wide range of options and opinions.

"The most important thing now is to avoid all-male leadership cultures," says Kim Campbell. Research on EI and gender shows that women tend to have stronger empathy and relationship skills than men do. "These strengths of women's leadership are not so much innate aspects of femininity as they are the result of disempowerment," says Campbell. Women developed them as means of survival in male-dominated cultures. Men can, of course, exhibit these skills too, just as women can demonstrate toughness and decisiveness. When there's sufficient trust on a leadership team, gender diversity can boost the team's ability to manage its own emotions and respond to those of others in the unit.

A Caveat

"When you're mobilizing people to engage in any kind of strategy, you're really asking them to sift through what they're not going to do," says Heifetz. If your heart is closed, he and coauthor Marty Linsky write in *Leadership on the Line*—if you lack the compassion, childlike innocence, and curiosity that enable you "to listen with open ears, and to embrace new and disturbing ideas"—then you "cannot fathom those stakes, or the losses people will have to sustain as they conserve what's most precious and learn how to thrive in the new environment." An open heart helps you lead people and organizations more effectively through change and loss. But it also makes you more vulnerable to the resistance and hostility that regularly accompany such losses.

"We tend to put a smiley face on leadership and talk about it in terms of inspiration, vision, and creativity," says Heifetz. "It is all those things, but it's also hard, painful, and dangerous. 'Staying in the game,' learning how to sustain yourself, is therefore one of the essential tasks of leadership."

For Further Reading

Primal Leadership: Realizing the Power of Emotional Intelligence by Daniel Goleman, Richard Boyatzis, and Annie McKee (2002, Harvard Business School Press)

Leadership on the Line: Staying Alive Through the Dangers of Leading by Ronald A. Heifetz and Marty Linsky (2002, Harvard Business School Press)

Reprint U0207B

About the Contributors

Nick Morgan is author of *Working the Room* (Harvard Business School Press, 2003).

Jennifer McFarland is a contributor to *Harvard Management Update*.

Lauren Keller Johnson is a business writer living in Harvard, Massachusetts.

David Stauffer is a contributor to *Harvard Management Update*.

Loren Gary is a contributor to *Harvard Management Update*.

Michael Watkins is associate professor of business administration at Harvard Business School, where he is a member of the Negotiation and Decision-Making faculty group. He is author of *The First 90 Days* (Harvard Business School Press, 2003).

John Baldoni is a consultant specializing in leadership communications and development, and is the author of *Personal Leadership* (Elsewhere Press, 2001).

Melissa Raffoni is a managing partner of ProfessionalSkills Alliance and on the faculty of MIT's Sloan School of Management, where she teaches a course on effective managerial communications

Harvard Business Review Paperback Series

The Harvard Business Review Paperback Series offers the best thinking on cutting-edge management ideas from the world's leading thinkers, researchers, and managers. Designed for leaders who believe in the power of ideas to change business, these books will be useful to managers at all levels of experience, but especially senior executives and general managers. In addition, this series is widely used in training and executive development programs.

Books are priced at $19.95 U.S.
Price subject to change.

Title	Product #
Harvard Business Review **Interviews with CEOs**	3294
Harvard Business Review on **Advances in Strategy**	8032
Harvard Business Review on **Becoming a High Performance Manager**	1296
Harvard Business Review on **Brand Management**	1445
Harvard Business Review on **Breakthrough Leadership**	8059
Harvard Business Review on **Breakthrough Thinking**	181X
Harvard Business Review on **Building Personal and Organizational Resilience**	2721
Harvard Business Review on **Business and the Environment**	2336
Harvard Business Review on **Change**	8842
Harvard Business Review on **Compensation**	701X
Harvard Business Review on **Corporate Ethics**	273X
Harvard Business Review on **Corporate Governance**	2379
Harvard Business Review on **Corporate Responsibility**	2748
Harvard Business Review on **Corporate Strategy**	1429
Harvard Business Review on **Crisis Management**	2352
Harvard Business Review on **Culture and Change**	8369
Harvard Business Review on **Customer Relationship Management**	6994
Harvard Business Review on **Decision Making**	5572
Harvard Business Review on **Effective Communication**	1437

Title	Product #
Harvard Business Review on **Entrepreneurship**	9105
Harvard Business Review on **Finding and Keeping the Best People**	5564
Harvard Business Review on **Innovation**	6145
Harvard Business Review on **Knowledge Management**	8818
Harvard Business Review on **Leadership**	8834
Harvard Business Review on **Leadership at the Top**	2756
Harvard Business Review on **Leading in Turbulent Times**	1806
Harvard Business Review on **Managing Diversity**	7001
Harvard Business Review on **Managing High-Tech Industries**	1828
Harvard Business Review on **Managing People**	9075
Harvard Business Review on **Managing the Value Chain**	2344
Harvard Business Review on **Managing Uncertainty**	9083
Harvard Business Review on **Managing Your Career**	1318
Harvard Business Review on **Marketing**	8040
Harvard Business Review on **Measuring Corporate Performance**	8826
Harvard Business Review on **Mergers and Acquisitions**	5556
Harvard Business Review on **Motivating People**	1326
Harvard Business Review on **Negotiation**	2360
Harvard Business Review on **Nonprofits**	9091
Harvard Business Review on **Organizational Learning**	6153
Harvard Business Review on **Strategic Alliances**	1334
Harvard Business Review on **Strategies for Growth**	8850
Harvard Business Review on **The Business Value of IT**	9121
Harvard Business Review on **The Innovative Enterprise**	130X
Harvard Business Review on **Turnarounds**	6366
Harvard Business Review on **What Makes a Leader**	6374
Harvard Business Review on **Work and Life Balance**	3286

Management Dilemmas:
Case Studies from the Pages of
Harvard Business Review

How often do you wish you could turn to a panel of experts to guide you through tough management situations? The Management Dilemmas series provides just that. Drawn from the pages of *Harvard Business Review,* each insightful volume poses several perplexing predicaments and shares the problem-solving wisdom of leading experts. Engagingly written, these solutions-oriented collections help managers make sound judgment calls when addressing everyday management dilemmas.

These books are priced at $19.95 U.S.
Price subject to change.

Title	Product #
Management Dilemmas: **When Change Comes Undone**	5038
Management Dilemmas: **When Good People Behave Badly**	5046
Management Dilemmas: **When Marketing Becomes a Minefield**	290X

Harvard Business Essentials

In the fast-paced world of business today, everyone needs a personal resource—a place to go for advice, coaching, background information, or answers. The Harvard Business Essentials series fits the bill. Concise and straightforward, these books provide highly practical advice for readers at all levels of experience. Whether you are a new manager interested in expanding your skills or an experienced executive looking to stay on top, these solution-oriented books give you the reliable tips and tools you need to improve your performance and get the job done. Harvard Business Essentials titles will quickly become your constant companions and trusted guides.

These books are priced at $19.95 U.S., except as noted.
Price subject to change.

Title	Product #
Harvard Business Essentials: **Negotiation**	1113
Harvard Business Essentials: **Managing Creativity and Innovation**	1121
Harvard Business Essentials: **Managing Change and Transition**	8741
Harvard Business Essentials: **Hiring and Keeping the Best People**	875X
Harvard Business Essentials: **Finance for Managers**	8768
Harvard Business Essentials: **Business Communication**	113X
Harvard Business Essentials: **Manager's Toolkit ($24.95)**	2896
Harvard Business Essentials: **Managing Projects Large and Small**	3213
Harvard Business Essentials: **Creating Teams with an Edge**	290X

The Results-Driven Manager

The Results-Driven Manager series collects timely articles from *Harvard Management Update* and *Harvard Management Communication Letter* to help senior to middle managers sharpen their skills, increase their effectiveness, and gain a competitive edge. Presented in a concise, accessible format to save managers valuable time, these books offer authoritative insights and techniques for improving job performance and achieving immediate results.

These books are priced at $14.95 U.S.
Price subject to change.

Readers of the Results-Driven Manager series find the following Harvard Business School Press books of interest.

If you find these books useful:	You may also like these:
Presentations That Persuade and Motivate	Working the Room (8199)
Getting People on Board	
Face-to-Face Communications for Clarity and Impact	HBR on Effective Communication (1437)
Dealing with Difficult People	HBR on Managing People (9075)
Winning Negotiations That Preserve Relationships	HBR on Negotiation (2360)
	HBE Guide to Negotiation (1113)
Teams That Click	The Wisdom of Teams (3670)
	Leading Teams (3332)
Managing Yourself for the Career You Want	Primal Leadership (486X)
	Leading Quietly (4878)
Taking Control of Your Time	Leadership on the Line (4371)

How to Order

Harvard Business School Press publications are available worldwide from your local bookseller or online retailer.
You can also call

1-800-668-6780

Our product consultants are available to help you
8:00 a.m.–6:00 p.m., Monday–Friday, Eastern Time.
Outside the U.S. and Canada, call: 617-783-7450
Please call about special discounts for quantities greater than ten.

You can order online at

www.HBSPress.org